70 COFFEE CAKES AND DESSERTS

70 COFFEE CAKES AND DESSERTS

Delectable mousses, ice creams, terrines, puddings, pies, pastries and cookies, shown step by step in more than 270 gorgeous photographs

CATHERINE ATKINSON

southwater

This edition is published by Southwater, an imprint of Anness Publishing Ltd,
Blaby Road, Wigston, Leicestershire LE18 4SE; info@anness.com

www.southwaterbooks.com; www.annesspublishing.com

If you like the images in this book and would like to investigate using them for publishing,
promotions or advertising, please visit our website www.practicalpictures.com for more information.

Publisher: Joanna Lorenz
Editor: Finny Fox-Davies
Designer: Ian Hunt
Photography: William Lingwood
Home Economy: Carol Tennant
Styling: Helen Trent
Production Controller: Wendy Lawson

© Anness Publishing Ltd 2013

NOTES

For all recipes, quantities are given in both metric and imperial measures and, where appropriate, in standard cups and spoons.
Follow one set of measures, but not a mixture, because they are not interchangeable.
Standard spoon and cup measures are level. 1 tsp = 5ml, 1 tbsp = 15ml, 1 cup = 250ml/8fl oz.
Australian standard tablespoons are 20ml. Australian readers should use 3 tsp in place of 1 tbsp for measuring small quantities.
American pints are 16fl oz/2 cups. American readers should use 20fl oz/2.5 cups in place of 1 pint when measuring liquids.
Electric oven temperatures in this book are for conventional ovens. When using a fan oven, the temperature will probably need to be
reduced by about 10–20°C/20–40°F. Since ovens vary, you should check with your manufacturer's instruction book for guidance.
Medium (US large) eggs are used unless otherwise stated.

CONTENTS

INTRODUCTION

THIS BOOK CONTAINS OVER 70 RECIPES PRESENTED IN A BEAUTIFULLY ILLUSTRATED STEP-BY-STEP FORMAT. ALL THE CLASSIC COFFEE RECIPES ARE INCLUDED, SUCH AS TIRAMISU, COFFEE COEURS À LA CRÈME, MOCHA SPONGE CAKE AND CAPPUCCINO TORTE. THERE ARE ALSO RECIPES FOR ALL OCCASIONS, FROM FRUIT AND FROZEN DESSERTS, SUMPTUOUS TORTES, RICH PIES AND PASTRIES AND IRRESISTIBLE COOKIES AND BREADS. ALL OF THE RECIPES DEMONSTRATE JUST HOW VERSATILE AN INGREDIENT COFFEE IS; IT COMBINES EFFORTLESSLY WITH SO MANY OTHER FLAVOURS, SUCH AS ALCOHOL, FRUIT, CHOCOLATE AND CREAM. ALWAYS USE GOOD-QUALITY COFFEE, AND EXPERIMENTING WITH COFFEES FROM AROUND THE WORLD WILL MAKE EACH DISH A DELICIOUS CULINARY ADVENTURE.

CREAM DESSERTS AND HOT PUDDINGS

Smooth creamy custards form the base of many cold desserts, such as Coffee Crème Caramel and Petits Pots de Cappuccino, as well as hot ones such as Apricot Panettone Pudding. Served in tall elegant glasses, light airy mousses feature frequently among the most memorable desserts. Many are also blissfully simple; such as Coffee Cardamom Zabaglione and Chocolate and Espresso Mousse.

CLASSIC COFFEE CRÈME CARAMEL

THESE LIGHTLY SET COFFEE CUSTARDS ARE SERVED IN A POOL OF CARAMEL SAUCE. FOR A RICHER FLAVOUR, MAKE THEM WITH HALF SINGLE CREAM, HALF MILK.

SERVES SIX

INGREDIENTS
    600ml/1 pint/2½ cups milk
    45ml/3 tbsp ground coffee
    50g/2oz/¼ cup caster sugar
    4 eggs
    4 egg yolks
    spun sugar, to decorate (optional)
For the caramel sauce
    150g/5oz/¾ cup caster sugar
    60ml/4 tbsp water

1 Preheat the oven to 160°C/325°F/ Gas 3. To make the caramel sauce, gently heat the sugar in a small heavy-based pan with the water, until the sugar has dissolved. Bring to the boil and boil rapidly until the syrup turns a rich golden brown.

5 Put the ramekins in a roasting tin and pour in enough hot water to come two-thirds of the way up the sides of the dishes. Bake for 30–35 minutes or until just set. Test by gently shaking one of the custards; it should wobble like a jelly. Remove the custards from the hot water and leave to cool.

6 Chill the coffee custards for at least 3 hours. To turn out, carefully loosen the sides with a palette knife then invert on to serving plates. Decorate with spun sugar, if using.

COOK'S TIP
To make spun sugar, gently heat 75g/ 3oz/scant ½ cup caster sugar, 5ml/1 tsp liquid glucose and 30ml/2 tbsp water in a heavy-based pan until the sugar dissolves. Boil the syrup to 160°C/325°F, then briefly dip the base of the pan into cold water. Put a sheet of greaseproof paper on the work surface to protect it. Holding two forks together, dip them into the syrup and flick them rapidly backwards and forwards over an oiled rolling pin. Store in an airtight container until ready to use.

2 Quickly and carefully, pour the hot syrup into six warmed 150ml/¼ pint/ ⅔ cup ramekins.

3 To make the coffee custard, heat the milk until almost boiling. Pour over the ground coffee and leave to infuse for about 5 minutes. Strain through a fine sieve into a jug.

4 In a bowl, whisk the caster sugar, eggs and yolks until light and creamy. Whisk the coffee-flavoured milk into the egg mixture. Pour into the ramekins.

TIRAMISU

THE NAME OF THIS CLASSIC DESSERT TRANSLATES AS "PICK ME UP", WHICH IS SAID TO DERIVE FROM THE FACT THAT IT IS SO GOOD THAT IT LITERALLY MAKES YOU SWOON WHEN YOU EAT IT.

SERVES FOUR

INGREDIENTS
  225g/8oz/1 cup mascarpone
  25g/1oz/¼ cup icing sugar, sifted
  150ml/¼ pint/⅔ cup strong brewed
    coffee, chilled
  300ml/½ pint/1¼ cups double cream
  45ml/3 tbsp coffee liqueur such as
    Tia Maria, Kahlúa or Toussaint
  115g/4oz Savoiardi (sponge
    finger) biscuits
  50g/2oz bittersweet or plain
    chocolate, coarsely grated
  cocoa powder, for dusting

1 Lightly grease and line a 900g/2lb loaf tin with clear film. Put the mascarpone and icing sugar in a large bowl and beat for 1 minute. Stir in 30ml/2 tbsp of the chilled coffee. Mix thoroughly.

2 Whip the cream with 15ml/1 tbsp of the liqueur until it forms soft peaks. Stir a spoonful into the mascarpone mixture, then fold in the rest. Spoon half the mascarpone mixture into the loaf tin and smooth the top.

3 Put the remaining strong brewed coffee and liqueur in a shallow dish just wider than the Savoiardi biscuits. Using half the biscuits, dip one side of each biscuit into the coffee mixture, then arrange on top of the mascarpone mixture in a single layer.

4 Spoon the rest of the mascarpone mixture over the biscuit layer and smooth the top.

5 Dip the remaining biscuits in the coffee mixture, and arrange on top. Drizzle any remaining coffee mixture over the top. Cover the dish with clear film and chill for at least 4 hours. Carefully turn the tiramisu out of the loaf tin and sprinkle with grated chocolate and cocoa powder; serve cut into slices.

COOK'S TIP
Mascarpone is a silky-textured, soft, thick cream cheese, originally from Lombardy, and made with cows' milk.

COFFEE CARDAMOM ZABAGLIONE

THIS WARM ITALIAN DESSERT IS USUALLY MADE WITH ITALIAN MARSALA WINE. IN THIS RECIPE COFFEE LIQUEUR IS USED ALONG WITH FRESHLY CRUSHED CARDAMOM.

SERVES FOUR

INGREDIENTS
4 cardamom pods
8 egg yolks
50g/2oz/4 tbsp golden caster sugar
30ml/2 tbsp strong brewed coffee
50ml/2fl oz/¼ cup coffee liqueur
  such as Tia Maria, Kahlúa
  or Toussaint
a few crushed roasted coffee beans,
  to decorate

1 Peel away the pale green outer husks from the cardamom pods and remove the black seeds. Crush these to a fine powder using a pestle and mortar.

2 Put the egg yolks, caster sugar and crushed cardamom seeds in a large bowl and whisk with an electric hand whisk for 1–2 minutes, or until the mixture is pale and creamy.

3 Gradually whisk the coffee and the liqueur into the egg yolk mixture.

4 Place the bowl over a saucepan of near-boiling water and continue whisking for about 10 minutes.

5 Continue whisking until the mixture is very thick and fluffy and has doubled in volume, making sure the water doesn't boil – if it does the mixture will curdle. Remove the bowl from the heat and carefully pour the zabaglione into four warmed glasses or dishes. Sprinkle with a few crushed roasted coffee beans and serve immediately.

COOK'S TIP
Cardamom is a fragrant spice from northern India. It may be bought ready-ground, but freshly crushed cardamom is much sweeter.

PETITS POTS DE CAPPUCCINO

THESE VERY RICH COFFEE CUSTARDS, WITH A CREAM TOPPING AND A LIGHT DUSTING OF DRINKING CHOCOLATE, LOOK WONDERFUL PRESENTED IN FINE CHINA COFFEE CUPS.

SERVES SIX TO EIGHT

INGREDIENTS
    75g/3oz/1 cup roasted coffee beans
    300ml/½ pint/1¼ cups milk
    300ml/½ pint/1¼ cups single cream
    1 whole egg
    4 egg yolks
    50g/2oz/4 tbsp caster sugar
    2.5ml/½ tsp vanilla extract
For the topping
    120ml/4fl oz/½ cup whipping cream
    45ml/3 tbsp iced water
    10ml/2 tsp drinking chocolate

1 Preheat the oven to 160°C/325°F/ Gas 3. Put the roasted coffee beans in a saucepan over a low heat for about 3 minutes, shaking the pan frequently.

2 Pour the milk and cream over the beans. Heat until almost boiling; cover and leave to infuse for 30 minutes.

3 Whisk the egg, the egg yolks, sugar and vanilla together. Return the milk to boiling and pour through a sieve on to the egg mixture. Discard the beans.

4 Pour the mixture into eight 75ml/ 5 tbsp coffee cups or six 120ml/4fl oz/ ½ cup ramekins. Cover each with a small piece of foil.

5 Put in a roasting tin with hot water reaching about two-thirds of the way up the sides of the dishes. Bake them for 30–35 minutes, or until lightly set. Let cool. Chill in the fridge for at least 2 hours.

6 Whisk the whipping cream and iced water until thick and frothy and spoon on top of the custards. Dust with drinking chocolate before serving.

COOK'S TIPS
These petits pots may also be served warm, topped with a spoonful of clotted cream. Serve straight away, with the clotted cream just starting to melt.

COFFEE AND BRANDY SYLLABUB

THIS HEAVENLY DESSERT COULDN'T BE EASIER — A FROTH OF WHIPPED COFFEE AND BRANDY CREAM TOPS JUICY GRAPES. CRISP BISCUITS ARE A DELICIOUS CONTRAST.

SERVES SIX

INGREDIENTS
   75g/3oz/6 tbsp soft light
      brown sugar
   finely grated rind of ½ orange
   120ml/4fl oz/½ cup brandy
   120ml/4fl oz/½ cup cold strong
      brewed coffee
   400ml/14fl oz/1⅔ cups double cream
   225g/8oz white seedless grapes
   sugared grapes, to decorate
   crisp biscuits, to serve

COOK'S TIP
For sugared grapes, wash and dry the fruit, then snip into small clusters. Use a fine brush to paint lightly beaten egg white evenly on to the grapes, then dust with caster sugar. Shake off excess sugar and leave to dry before using.

1 Put the brown sugar, orange rind and brandy into a small bowl. Stir well, then cover with clear film and leave to stand for 1 hour.

2 Strain the mixture through a fine sieve into a clean bowl. Stir in the coffee. Slowly pour in the cream, whisking all the time.

3 Continue whisking for 3–4 minutes, until the mixture thickens enough to stand in soft peaks.

4 Divide the grapes between the glasses. Pour or spoon the syllabub over the grapes. Chill in the fridge for 1 hour. Decorate the glasses with clusters of sugared grapes and serve with crisp biscuits.

COFFEE JELLIES

SERVE THESE SPARKLING COFFEE JELLIES AS A LIGHT AND REFRESHING END TO A RICH MEAL.

SERVES FOUR

INGREDIENTS
   20ml/4 tsp powdered gelatine
   75ml/5 tbsp cold water
   600ml/1 pint/2½ cups very hot strong
      brewed coffee
   40g/1½oz/3 tbsp caster sugar
For the bay cream
   300ml/½ pint/1¼ cups
      whipping cream
   15ml/1 tbsp bay-scented caster sugar
   fresh bay leaves, to decorate

VARIATION
For a creamy version of these jellies, make the coffee with hot milk and serve with fresh fruit instead of bay cream.

COOK'S TIP
To make bay-scented caster sugar, add 2–3 dried bay leaves to caster sugar. Leave for at least a week before using.

1 To make the jellies, sprinkle the gelatine over the cold water. Leave to soak for 2–3 minutes. Add to the hot strong brewed coffee with the sugar and stir to dissolve.

2 Allow the coffee to cool, then pour into four 150ml/¼ pint/⅔ cup metal moulds. Chill in the fridge for 3 hours or until set.

3 To make the bay cream, lightly whisk the cream and bay scented caster sugar until very soft peaks form. Spoon into a serving bowl.

4 To serve, dip the moulds in a bowl of hot water for a few seconds, then invert on to individual serving plates. Serve with the bay cream and decorate with fresh bay leaves.

COFFEE COEUR À LA CRÈME

THESE PRETTY HEART-SHAPED CREAMS, SPECKLED WITH ESPRESSO-ROASTED COFFEE BEANS, ARE SERVED WITH A FRESH FRUIT SAUCE. USE WILD STRAWBERRIES, IF AVAILABLE, FOR THEIR WONDERFUL PERFUME.

SERVES SIX

INGREDIENTS
    25g/1oz/generous ¼ cup espresso-
        roasted coffee beans
    225g/8oz/1 cup ricotta or
        curd cheese
    300ml/½ pint/1¼ cups crème fraîche
    25g/1oz/2 tbsp caster sugar
    finely grated rind of ½ orange
    2 egg whites
For the red fruit coulis
    175g/6oz/1 cup raspberries
    30ml/2 tbsp icing sugar, sifted
    115g/4oz/⅔ cup small strawberries,
        (or wild ones, if available), halved

1 Preheat the oven to 180°C/350°F/ Gas 4. Evenly spread the espresso-roasted coffee beans on to a baking sheet and toast for about 10 minutes. Allow to cool, then put in a large plastic bag and crush into tiny pieces with a rolling pin.

2 Thoroughly rinse 12 pieces of muslin in cold water and squeeze dry. Use to line six coeur à la crème moulds with a double layer, allowing the muslin to overhang the edges.

3 Press the ricotta or curd cheese through a fine sieve into a bowl. Stir the crème fraîche, sugar, orange rind and crushed roasted coffee beans together. Add to the cheese and mix well.

4 Whisk the egg whites until stiff and fold into the mixture. Spoon into the prepared moulds, then bring the muslin up and over the filling. Leave in the fridge overnight to drain and chill.

5 To make the red fruit coulis, put the raspberries and icing sugar in a food processor and blend until smooth. Push through a fine sieve to remove the pips. Stir in the strawberries. Chill until ready to serve.

6 Unmould the hearts on to individual serving plates and carefully remove the muslin. Spoon the red fruit coulis over before serving.

COOK'S TIP
Muslin has a fine weave which allows the liquid from the cheese to drain through. If you haven't got any muslin, use a new all-purpose disposable cloth instead.

CHILLED CHOCOLATE AND ESPRESSO MOUSSE

HEADY, AROMATIC ESPRESSO COFFEE ADDS A DISTINCTIVE FLAVOUR TO THIS SMOOTH, RICH MOUSSE.
SERVE IT IN STYLISH CHOCOLATE CUPS FOR A SPECIAL OCCASION.

SERVES FOUR

INGREDIENTS
    225g/8oz plain chocolate
    45ml/3 tbsp brewed espresso
    25g/1oz/2 tbsp unsalted butter
    4 eggs, separated
    sprigs of fresh mint,
        to decorate (optional)
    mascarpone or clotted cream,
        to serve (optional)
For the chocolate cups
    225g/8oz plain chocolate

1 For each chocolate cup, cut a double thickness 15cm/6in square of foil. Mould it around a small orange, leaving the edges and corners loose to make a cup shape. Remove the orange and press the bottom of the foil case gently on a surface to make a flat base. Repeat to make four foil cups.

2 Break the plain chocolate into small pieces and place in a bowl set over a pan of very hot water. Stir occasionally until the chocolate has melted.

3 Spoon the chocolate into the foil cups, spreading it up the sides with the back of a spoon to give a ragged edge. Refrigerate for 30 minutes or until set hard. Gently peel away the foil, starting at the top edge.

4 To make the chocolate mousse, put the plain chocolate and brewed espresso into a bowl set over a pan of hot water and melt as before. When it is smooth and liquid, add the unsalted butter, a little at a time. Remove the pan from the heat then stir in the egg yolks.

5 Whisk the egg whites in a bowl until stiff, but not dry, then fold them into the chocolate mixture. Pour into a bowl and refrigerate for at least 3 hours.

6 To serve, scoop the chilled mousse into the chocolate cups. Add a scoop of mascarpone or clotted cream and decorate with a sprig of fresh mint, if you wish.

APRICOT PANETTONE PUDDING

SLICES OF LIGHT-TEXTURED PANETTONE ARE LAYERED WITH DRIED APRICOTS AND COOKED IN A CREAMY COFFEE CUSTARD FOR A SATISFYINGLY WARMING DESSERT.

SERVES FOUR

INGREDIENTS

50g/2oz/4 tbsp unsalted
   butter, softened
6 x 1cm/½in thick slices (about
   400g/14oz) panettone containing
   candied fruit
175g/6oz/¾ cup ready-to-eat dried
   apricots, chopped
400ml/14fl oz/1⅔ cups milk
250ml/8fl oz/1 cup double cream
60ml/4 tbsp mild-flavoured
   ground coffee
90g/3½oz/½ cup caster sugar
3 eggs
30ml/2 tbsp demerara sugar
pouring cream or crème fraîche,
   to serve

1 Preheat the oven to 160°C/325°F/ Gas 3. Brush a 2 litre/3½ pint/8 cup oval baking dish with 15g/½oz/1 tbsp of the butter. Spread the panettone with the remaining butter and arrange in the baking dish. Cut to fit and scatter the apricots among and over the layers.

2 Pour the milk and cream into a pan and heat until almost boiling. Pour the milk mixture over the coffee and leave to infuse for 10 minutes. Strain through a fine sieve, discarding the coffee grounds.

3 Lightly beat the caster sugar and eggs together, then whisk in the warm coffee-flavoured milk. Slowly pour the mixture over the panettone. Leave to soak for 15 minutes.

4 Sprinkle the top of the pudding with demerara sugar and place the dish in a large roasting tin. Pour in enough boiling water to come halfway up the sides of the baking dish.

5 Bake for 40–45 minutes until the top is golden and crusty, but the middle still slightly wobbly. Remove from the oven, but leave the dish in the hot water for 10 minutes. Serve warm with pouring cream or crème fraîche.

COOK'S TIP
This recipe works equally well with plain or chocolate-flavoured panettone.

STICKY COFFEE AND GINGER PUDDING

THIS COFFEE-CAPPED FEATHER-LIGHT SPONGE IS MADE WITH BREADCRUMBS AND GROUND ALMONDS.
SERVE WITH CREAMY CUSTARD OR SCOOPS OF VANILLA ICE CREAM.

SERVES FOUR

INGREDIENTS
30ml/2 tbsp soft light brown sugar
25g/1oz/2 tbsp stem ginger, chopped
30ml/2 tbsp mild-flavoured
    ground coffee
75ml/5 tbsp stem ginger syrup (from
    a jar of stem ginger)
115g/4oz/generous ½ cup
    caster sugar
3 eggs, separated
25g/1oz/¼ cup plain flour
5ml/1 tsp ground ginger
65g/2½oz/generous 1 cup fresh
    white breadcrumbs
25g/1oz/¼ cup ground almonds

1 Preheat the oven to 180°C/350°F/ Gas 4. Grease and line the base of a 750ml/1¼ pint/3 cup pudding basin, then sprinkle in the soft light brown sugar and chopped stem ginger.

2 Put the ground coffee in a small bowl. Heat the ginger syrup until almost boiling; pour into the coffee. Stir well and leave for 4 minutes. Pour through a fine sieve into the pudding basin.

3 Beat half the caster sugar and egg yolks until light and fluffy. Sift the flour and ground ginger together and fold into the egg mixture with the breadcrumbs and ground almonds.

4 Whisk the egg whites until stiff, then gradually whisk in the remaining caster sugar. Fold into the mixture, half at a time. Spoon into the pudding basin and smooth the top.

5 Cover the basin with a piece of pleated greased greaseproof paper and secure with string. Bake for 40 minutes, or until the sponge is firm to the touch. Turn out and serve immediately.

COOK'S TIP
This pudding can also be baked in a 900ml/1½ pint/3¾ cup loaf tin and served thickly sliced.

SOUFFLÉS AND MERINGUES

Fluffy soufflés that rise to the occasion and melt-in-the-mouth meringues — these are coffee desserts to tempt your eye and your palate. The basic ingredients for meringues couldn't be simpler — just egg whites and sugar, to which coffee lends a sophisticated touch. For the perfect finish to a meal, try spicy Floating Islands, or the tropical taste of Mango and Coffee Meringue Roll.

CHILLED COFFEE AND PRALINE SOUFFLÉ

A SMOOTH COFFEE SOUFFLÉ WITH A CRUSHED PRALINE TOPPING THAT IS SPECTACULAR AND EASY.

<u>SERVES SIX</u>

INGREDIENTS
   150g/5oz/¾ cup caster sugar
   75ml/5 tbsp water
   150g/5oz/generous 1 cup blanched
     almonds, plus extra, for decoration
   120ml/4fl oz/½ cup strong brewed
     coffee, e.g. hazelnut-flavoured
   15ml/1 tbsp powdered gelatine
   3 eggs, separated
   75g/3oz/scant ½ cup soft light
     brown sugar
   15ml/1 tbsp coffee liqueur, such as
     Tia Maria, Kahlúa or Toussaint
   150ml/¼ pint/⅔ cup double cream
   about 150ml/¼ pint/⅔ cup double
     cream, for decoration (optional)

1 Cut a paper collar from a double layer of greaseproof paper, 5cm/2in deeper than a 900ml/1½ pint/3¾ cup soufflé dish. Wrap around the dish and tie in place with string. Refrigerate.

2 Oil a baking sheet. Put the caster sugar in a small heavy-based pan with the water and heat gently until the sugar dissolves. Boil rapidly until the syrup becomes pale golden. Add the almonds and boil until dark golden.

3 Pour the mixture on to the baking sheet and leave to set. When hard, transfer to a plastic bag and break into pieces with a rolling pin. Reserve 50g/2oz/½ cup and crush the remainder.

4 Pour half the coffee into a small bowl; sprinkle over the gelatine. Leave to soak for 5 minutes, then place the bowl over a pan of hot water; stir until dissolved.

5 Put the egg yolks, soft light brown sugar, remaining coffee and liqueur in a bowl over a pan of simmering water. Whisk until thick and foamy, then whisk in the dissolved gelatine.

6 Whip the cream until soft peaks form, then whisk the egg whites until stiff. Fold the crushed praline into the cream, then fold into the coffee mixture. Finally, fold in the egg whites, half at a time.

7 Spoon into the soufflé dish and smooth the top; chill for at least 2 hours or until set. Put in the freezer for 15–20 minutes before serving. Remove the paper collar by running a warmed palette knife between the set soufflé and the paper. Whisk the cream for decoration, if using, and place large spoonfuls on top. Decorate with the reserved praline pieces and whole blanched almonds.

TWICE-BAKED MOCHA SOUFFLÉ

THE PERFECT WAY TO END A MEAL, THESE MINI MOCHA SOUFFLÉS CAN BE MADE UP TO 3 HOURS AHEAD, THEN REHEATED JUST BEFORE YOU SERVE THEM.

SERVES SIX

INGREDIENTS
   75g/3oz/6 tbsp unsalted
      butter, softened
   90g/3½ oz bittersweet or
      plain chocolate, grated
   30ml/2 tbsp ground coffee
   400ml/14fl oz/1⅔ cup milk
   40g/1½oz/⅓ cup plain flour, sifted
   15g/½ oz/2 tbsp cocoa, sifted
   3 eggs, separated
   50g/2oz/¼ cup caster sugar
   175ml/6fl oz/¾ cup creamy
      chocolate or coffee liqueur, such as
      Crème de Caçao, Sheridans

1 Preheat the oven to 200°C/400°F/ Gas 6. Thickly brush six 150ml/¼ pint/ ⅔ cup dariole moulds or mini pudding basins with 25g/1oz/2 tbsp of the butter. Coat with 50g/2oz of the grated chocolate.

2 Put the ground coffee in a small bowl. Heat the milk until almost boiling and pour over the coffee. Infuse for 4 minutes and strain, discarding the grounds.

3 Melt the remaining butter in a small pan. Stir in the flour and cocoa to make a roux. Cook for about 1 minute, then gradually add the coffee milk, stirring all the time to make a very thick sauce. Simmer for 2 minutes. Remove from the heat and stir in the egg yolks.

VARIATION
Good quality white or milk cooking chocolate can be use instead of plain, if preferred.

4 Cool for 5 minutes, then stir in the remaining chocolate. Whisk the egg whites until stiff, then gradually whisk in the sugar. Stir half into the sauce to loosen, then fold in the remainder.

5 Spoon the mixture into the dariole moulds and place in a roasting tin. Pour in enough hot water to come two-thirds of the way up the sides of the tins.

6 Bake the soufflés for 15 minutes. Turn them out on to a baking tray and leave to cool completely.

7 Before serving, spoon 15ml/1 tbsp chocolate or coffee liqueur over each pudding and reheat in the oven for 6–7 minutes. Serve on individual plates with the remaining liqueur poured over.

Classic Chocolate and Coffee Roulade

This rich, squidgy chocolate roll should be made at least 12 hours before serving, to allow it to soften. Expect the roulade to crack a little when you roll it up.

SERVES EIGHT

INGREDIENTS
  200g/7oz plain chocolate
  200g/7oz/1 cup caster sugar
  7 eggs, separated
For the filling
  300ml/½ pint/1¼ cups double cream
  30ml/2 tbsp cold strong brewed
    coffee, e.g. mocha-flavoured
  15ml/1 tbsp coffee liqueur, such as
    Tia Maria, Kahlúa or Toussaint
  60ml/4 tbsp icing sugar, for dusting
  little grated chocolate, for sprinkling

1 Preheat the oven to 180°C/350°F/ Gas 4. Grease and line a 33 x 23cm/ 13 x 9in Swiss roll tin with non-stick baking parchment.

2 Break the chocolate into squares and melt in a bowl over a pan of barely simmering water. Remove from the heat and leave to cool for 5 minutes.

3 In a large bowl, whisk the sugar and egg yolks until light and fluffy. Stir in the melted chocolate.

4 Whisk the egg whites until stiff, but not dry, and then gently fold into the chocolate mixture.

5 Pour the chocolate mixture into the prepared tin, spreading it level with a spatula. Bake for about 25 minutes until firm. Leave the cake in the tin and cover with a cooling rack, making sure it doesn't touch the cake.

6 Cover the rack with a damp tea towel, then wrap in clear film. Leave in a cool place for at least 8 hours or overnight, if possible.

7 Dust a large sheet of greaseproof paper with icing sugar and turn out the roulade on to it. Peel off the lining.

8 To make the filling, whip the double cream with the coffee and liqueur until soft peaks form. Spread the cream over the roulade. Starting from one of the short ends, carefully roll it up, using the paper to help.

9 Place the roulade, seam-side down, on to a serving plate; dust generously with icing sugar and sprinkle with a little grated chocolate before serving.

COOK'S TIP
If liked, decorate the roulade with swirls of whipped cream and chocolate coffee beans or with clusters of raspberries and mint leaves.

MANGO AND COFFEE MERINGUE ROLL

A LIGHT AND FLUFFY ROLL OF MERINGUE IS THE IDEAL CONTRAST TO THE UNSWEETENED FILLING OF COFFEE, MASCARPONE AND JUICY RIPE MANGO.

SERVES SIX TO EIGHT

INGREDIENTS
  4 egg whites
  225g/8oz/generous 1 cup
    caster sugar
For the filling
  45ml/3 tbsp strong-flavoured
    ground coffee
  75ml/5 tbsp milk
  350g/12oz/1½ cups mascarpone
  1 ripe mango, cut into
    1cm/½in cubes

COOK'S TIP
If you like, the meringue can be sprinkled with 50g/2oz/½ cup of skinned chopped hazelnuts before baking.

1 Preheat the oven to 190°C/375°F/Gas 5. Line a 33 x 23cm/13 x 9in Swiss roll tin with lightly greased non-stick baking parchment. Whisk the egg whites until stiff. Gradually add the sugar, whisking after each addition until thick and glossy.

2 When the meringue is thick and glossy, spoon it into the prepared tin and smooth the surface. Bake for 15 minutes or until firm and golden.

3 Turn the meringue out on to a sheet of non-stick baking parchment. Remove the lining paper and leave until cold.

4 To make the filling, put the coffee in a small bowl. Heat the milk until it is nearly boiling and pour over the coffee. Leave to infuse for 4 minutes, then strain through a fine sieve, discarding the coffee grounds.

5 Beat the mascarpone until soft, then gradually beat in the coffee. Spread over the meringue, then scatter with the chopped mango.

6 Gently roll up the meringue from one of the short ends, with the help of the baking parchment. Transfer to a serving plate seam-side down. Chill for at least 30 minutes before serving.

GINGERED COFFEE MERINGUES

*WHAT COULD BE MORE ENTICING THAN TO BREAK THROUGH THE COATING OF CRISP MERINGUE TO
REVEAL JUST-MELTING COFFEE ICE CREAM ON A MOIST GINGER SPONGE?*

SERVES SIX

INGREDIENTS
    275g/10oz bought ginger cake
    600ml/1 pint/2½ cups coffee
        ice cream
    4 egg whites
    1.5ml/¼ tsp cream of tartar
    150g/5oz/¾ cup caster sugar
    25g/1oz/2 tbsp preserved ginger,
        finely chopped

1 Preheat the oven to 230°C/450°F/
Gas 8. Cut the ginger cake lengthways
into three slices. Stamp out two rounds
from each slice, using a 5cm/2in cutter,
and put on a baking tray.

2 Top each cake round with a large
scoop of coffee ice cream, then place
the baking tray in the freezer for at least
30 minutes.

3 Whisk the egg whites and cream of
tartar until soft peaks form. Gradually
add the sugar and continue whisking
until the mixture forms stiff peaks. Fold
in the preserved ginger.

4 Carefully spoon the meringue and
ginger mixture into a piping bag fitted
with a large plain nozzle.

COOK'S TIP
The ice cream is insulated in the oven by
the tiny bubbles of air in the meringue,
so ensure it is completely covered. Once
coated, the ice cream cakes could be
frozen until ready to cook.

5 Quickly pipe the meringue over the
ice cream, starting from the base and
working up to the top.

6 Bake in the oven for 3–4 minutes,
until the outside of the meringue is
crisp and lightly tinged with brown.
Serve immediately.

FLOATING ISLANDS

THIS WELL-KNOWN DESSERT GETS ITS NAME FROM THE POACHED MERINGUES SURROUNDED BY A "SEA" OF CRÈME ANGLAISE. THIS VERSION IS GIVEN A TOUCH OF THE EXOTIC THROUGH THE ADDITION OF STAR ANISE AND IS SERVED WITH A RICH COFFEE SAUCE.

SERVES SIX

INGREDIENTS
For the coffee crème Anglaise
    150ml/¼ pint/⅔ cup milk
    150ml/¼ pint/⅔ cup single cream
    120ml/4fl oz/½ cup strong
      brewed coffee
    4 egg yolks
    25g/1oz/2 tbsp soft light
      brown sugar
    5ml/1 tsp cornflour
For the caramel sauce
    90g/3½oz/½ cup caster sugar
For the poached meringues
    2 egg whites
    50g/2oz/¼ cup caster sugar
    1.5ml/¼ tsp ground star anise
    pinch of salt

1 To make the coffee crème Anglaise, pour the milk, cream and coffee into a pan and heat to boiling point.

2 In a large bowl, whisk the egg yolks, brown sugar and cornflour together until creamy. Whisk in the hot coffee mixture, then pour the entire mixture back into the pan.

3 Heat for 1–2 minutes, stirring until the sauce thickens. Take off the heat and allow to cool, stirring occasionally.

COOK'S TIP
Once poached, the meringues will keep their shape for up to 2 hours.

4 Cover the bowl containing the sauce with clear film and place in the fridge.

5 For the caramel, put the sugar in a small heavy-based pan with 45ml/3 tbsp water and heat very gently until dissolved. Boil rapidly until the syrup turns a rich golden colour. Off the heat, carefully add 45ml/3 tbsp hot water – it will splutter. Leave to cool.

6 To make the meringues, whisk the egg whites until stiff. Combine the sugar and star anise; add to the egg whites.

7 Pour 2.5cm/1in of boiling water into a large frying pan. Add the salt and bring to a gentle simmer. Shape the meringue into small ovals, using two spoons, and add to the water. Poach four or five of the meringues at a time for about 3 minutes, until firm.

8 Remove with a slotted spoon and drain on kitchen paper. Repeat with the remaining mixture.

9 To serve, spoon a little coffee crème Anglaise on to each serving plate. Float two or three "islands" on top, then drizzle with caramel sauce.

COFFEE MERINGUES ᵂᴵᵀᴴ ROSE CREAM

THESE SUGARY MERINGUES, WITH CRUSHED ESPRESSO-ROASTED COFFEE BEANS, ARE FILLED WITH A DELICATE ROSE-SCENTED CREAM. LIGHTLY SPRINKLE ROSE PETALS FOR A ROMANTIC FINISH.

MAKES TWENTY PAIRS OF MERINGUES

INGREDIENTS
   25g/1oz/generous ¼ cup espresso-
     roasted coffee beans
   3 egg whites
   175g/6oz/scant 1 cup caster sugar
   25g/1oz/¼ cup pistachio nuts,
     roughly chopped
   few rose petals, for decoration
For the rose cream
   300ml/½ pint/1¼ cups double cream
   15ml/1 tbsp icing sugar, sifted
   10ml/2 tsp rose water

1 Preheat the oven to 180°C/350°F/ Gas 4. Spread the coffee beans on a baking sheet and toast for 8 minutes. Allow to cool, then put in a plastic bag and crush with a rolling pin. Turn the oven to 140°C/275°F/Gas 1.

2 Whisk the egg whites and sugar in a bowl over a pan of hot water until thick.

3 Remove from the heat and continue whisking until the meringue holds stiff peaks. Whisk in the crushed beans.

4 Fill a piping bag fitted with a large star nozzle with the mixture and pipe about 40 small swirls on to two baking sheets lined with non-stick baking parchment. Leave some space between each swirl.

5 Sprinkle with the pistachio nuts. Bake the meringues for 2–2½ hours, or until dry and crisp, swapping the position of the baking trays halfway through the cooking time. Leave to cool, then remove from the paper.

6 To make the rose cream, whip the cream, icing sugar and rose water until soft peaks form. Use to sandwich the meringues together in pairs. Arrange on a serving plate and serve scattered with rose petals for decoration.

VARIATION
Orange-flower water may be used instead of rose water in the cream and a drop of pink food colouring added, if you like.

COFFEE PAVLOVA <u>WITH</u> EXOTIC FRUITS

BOTH AUSTRALIA AND NEW ZEALAND CLAIM TO HAVE INVENTED THIS FLUFFY MERINGUE NAMED AFTER THE BALLERINA ANNA PAVLOVA. THE SECRET OF SUCCESS IS TO LEAVE THE MERINGUE IN THE OVEN UNTIL COMPLETELY COOLED, AS A SUDDEN CHANGE IN TEMPERATURE WILL MAKE IT CRACK.

SERVES SIX TO EIGHT

INGREDIENTS
   30ml/2 tbsp ground coffee,
     e.g. mocha orange-flavoured
   30ml/2 tbsp near-boiling water
   3 egg whites
   2.5ml/½ tsp cream of tartar
   175g/6oz/scant 1 cup caster sugar
   5ml/1 tsp cornflour, sifted
For the filling
   150ml/¼ pint/⅔ cup double cream
   5ml/1 tsp vanilla orange-flower water
   150ml/¼ pint/⅔ cup crème fraîche
   500g/1¼lb sliced exotic fruits, such
     as mango, papaya and kiwi
   15ml/1 tbsp icing sugar

4 Using a long knife or spatula, spoon the meringue mixture on to the baking sheet, spreading to an even 20cm/8in circle. Make a slight hollow in the middle. Bake in the oven for 1 hour, then turn off the heat and leave in the oven until cool.

5 Transfer the meringue to a plate, peeling off the lining. To make the filling, whip the cream with the orange-flower water until soft peaks form. Fold in the crème fraîche. Spoon into the meringue. Arrange the fruits over the cream and dust with icing sugar.

1 Preheat the oven to 140°C/275°F/ Gas 1. Draw a 20cm/8in circle on non-stick baking parchment. Place pencil-side down on a baking sheet.

2 Put the coffee in a small bowl and pour the hot water over. Leave to infuse for 4 minutes, then strain through a very fine sieve.

3 Whisk the egg whites with the cream of tartar until stiff, but not dry. Gradually whisk in the sugar until the meringue is stiff and shiny, then quickly whisk in the cornflour and coffee.

VARIATION
450g/1lb soft fruit, such as wild or cultivated strawberries, raspberries and blueberries, may be used instead of the exotic fruits, if you wish.

FRUIT
DESSERTS

*If you're looking for colour, flavour
and freshness and something
a little out of the ordinary, opt for
one of these fruit and coffee combi-
nations. Fruit always makes the
perfect pudding, no matter how simple or grand the meal, but it doesn't
have to be chilled. Try steeping
oranges in a hot coffee syrup or
serve a slice of Sticky Pear Pudding
for pure indulgence.*

ORANGES IN HOT COFFEE SYRUP

THIS RECIPE WORKS WELL WITH MOST CITRUS FRUITS; TRY PINK GRAPEFRUIT OR SWEET, PERFUMED CLEMENTINES, PEELED BUT LEFT WHOLE, FOR A CHANGE.

SERVES SIX

INGREDIENTS
  6 medium oranges
  200g/7oz/1 cup sugar
  50ml/2fl oz/¼ cup cold water
  100ml/3½fl oz/scant ½ cup
    boiling water
  100ml/3½fl oz/scant ½ cup fresh
    strong brewed coffee
  50g/2oz/½ cup pistachio nuts,
    chopped (optional)

COOK'S TIP
Choose a pan in which the oranges will just fit in a single layer.

1 Finely pare the rind from one orange, shred and reserve the rind. Peel the remaining oranges. Cut each one crosswise into slices, then re-form with a cocktail stick through the centre.

2 Put the sugar and cold water in a heavy-based pan. Heat gently until the sugar dissolves, then bring to the boil and cook until the syrup turns pale gold.

3 Remove from the heat and carefully pour the boiling water into the pan. Return to the heat until the syrup has dissolved in the water. Stir in the coffee.

4 Add the oranges and the shredded rind to the coffee syrup. Simmer for 15–20 minutes, turning the oranges once during cooking. Sprinkle with pistachio nuts, if using, and serve hot.

FRESH FIG COMPOTE

LIGHTLY POACHING FIGS IN A VANILLA AND COFFEE SYRUP BRINGS OUT THEIR WONDERFUL FLAVOUR.

SERVES FOUR TO SIX

INGREDIENTS
  400ml/14fl oz/1⅔ cups
    brewed coffee
  115g/4oz/½ cup clear honey
  1 vanilla pod
  12 slightly under-ripe
    fresh figs
  Greek yogurt, to serve (optional)

COOK'S TIPS
• Rinse and dry the vanilla pod; it can be used several times.
• Figs come in three main varieties – red, white and black – and all three are suitable for cooking. Naturally high in sugar, they are sweet and succulent and complement well the stronger flavours of coffee and vanilla.

1 Choose a frying pan with a lid, large enough to hold the figs in a single layer. Pour in the coffee and add the honey.

2 Split the vanilla pod lengthways and scrape the seeds into the pan. Add the vanilla pod, then bring to the boil. Bring the syrup to a rapid boil and cook until reduced to about 175ml/6fl oz/¾ cup. Leave to cool.

3 Wash the figs and pierce the skins several times with a sharp skewer. Cut in half and add to the syrup. Lower the heat, cover and simmer for 5 minutes. Remove the figs from the syrup with a slotted spoon and set aside to cool.

4 Strain the syrup over the figs. Allow to stand at room temperature for 1 hour before serving with yogurt, if liked.

STICKY PEAR PUDDING

CLOVES ADD A DISTINCTIVE FRAGRANT FLAVOUR TO THIS HAZELNUT, PEAR AND COFFEE PUDDING.

SERVES SIX

INGREDIENTS
30ml/2 tbsp ground coffee,
   e.g. hazelnut-flavoured
15ml/1 tbsp near-boiling water
50g/2oz/½ cup toasted
   skinned hazelnuts
4 ripe pears
juice of ½ orange
115g/4oz/8 tbsp butter, softened
115g/4oz/generous ½ cup golden
   caster sugar, plus an extra 15ml/
   1 tbsp, for baking
2 eggs, beaten
50g/2oz/½ cup self-raising
   flour, sifted
pinch of ground cloves
8 whole cloves, optional
45ml/3 tbsp maple syrup
fine strips of orange rind,
   to decorate
For the orange cream
300ml/½ pint/1¼ cups
   whipping cream
15ml/1 tbsp icing sugar, sifted
finely grated rind of ½ orange

1 Preheat the oven to 180°C/350°F/
Gas 4. Lightly grease a 20cm/8in loose-based sandwich tin. Put the ground coffee in a small bowl and pour the water over. Leave to infuse for 4 minutes, then strain through a fine sieve.

COOK'S TIP
If you can't find ready-toasted skinned hazelnuts, prepare your own. Toast under a hot grill for 3–4 minutes, turning frequently until well browned. Rub off the skins and cool before grinding.

2 Grind the hazelnuts in a coffee grinder until fine. Peel, halve and core the pears. Thinly slice across the pear halves part of the way through. Brush with orange juice.

3 Beat the butter and the 115g/4oz/
generous ½ cup caster sugar together in a large bowl until very light and fluffy. Gradually beat in the eggs, then fold in the flour, ground cloves, hazelnuts and coffee. Spoon the mixture into the tin and level the surface.

4 Pat the pears dry on kitchen paper, then arrange in the sponge mixture, flat side down.

5 Lightly press 2 whole cloves into each pear half, if using. Brush the pears with 15ml/1 tbsp maple syrup.

6 Sprinkle the pears with the 15ml/
1 tbsp caster sugar. Bake for 45–50 minutes or until firm and well-risen.

7 While the sponge is cooking, make the orange cream. Whip the cream, icing sugar and orange rind until soft peaks form. Spoon into a serving dish and chill until needed.

8 Allow the sponge to cool for about 10 minutes in the tin, then remove and place on a serving plate. Lightly brush with the remaining maple syrup before decorating with orange rind and serving warm with the orange cream.

COFFEE CRÊPES WITH PEACHES AND CREAM

JUICY GOLDEN PEACHES AND CREAM CONJURE UP THE SWEET TASTE OF SUMMER. HERE THEY ARE DELICIOUS AS THE FILLING FOR THESE LIGHT COFFEE CRÊPES.

SERVES SIX

INGREDIENTS
    75g/3oz/⅔ cup plain flour
    25g/1oz/¼ cup buckwheat flour
    1.5ml/¼ tsp salt
    1 egg, beaten
    200ml/7fl oz/scant 1 cup milk
    15g/½oz/1 tbsp butter, melted
    100ml/3½ oz/scant ½ cup strong
      brewed coffee
    sunflower oil, for frying
For the filling
    6 ripe peaches
    300ml/½ pint/1¼ cups double cream
    15ml/1 tbsp Amaretto liqueur
    225g/8oz/1 cup mascarpone
    65g/2½oz/generous ¼ cup
      caster sugar
    30ml/2 tbsp icing sugar, for dusting

1 Sift the flours and salt into a mixing bowl. Make a well in the middle and add the egg, half the milk and the melted butter. Gradually mix in the flour, beating until smooth, then beat in the remaining milk and coffee.

2 Heat a drizzle of oil in a 15–20cm/ 6–8in crêpe pan. Pour in just enough batter to thinly cover the base of the pan. Cook for 2–3 minutes, until the underneath is golden brown, then flip over and cook the other side.

COOK'S TIP
To keep the pancakes warm while you make the rest, cover them with foil and place the plate over a pan of barely simmering water.

3 Slide the crêpe out of the pan on to a plate. Continue making crêpes until all the mixture is used, stacking and interleaving with greaseproof paper.

4 To make the filling, halve the peaches and remove the stones. Cut into thick slices. Whip the cream and Amaretto liqueur until soft peaks form. Beat the mascarpone with the sugar until smooth. Beat 30ml/2 tbsp of the cream into the mascarpone, then fold in the remainder.

5 Spoon a little of the Amaretto cream on to one half of each pancake and top with peach slices. Gently fold the pancake over and dust with icing sugar. Serve immediately.

PLUM AND RUM BABAS

A POLISH KING THOUGHT UP THESE SPONGY YEAST CAKES AFTER HEARING THE STORY OF ALI BABA.
SOAKED IN A COFFEE AND RUM SYRUP, THEIR MIDDLES ARE FILLED WITH JUICY PLUMS.

SERVES SIX

INGREDIENTS

65g/2½oz/5 tbsp unsalted
  butter, softened
115g/4oz/1 cup strong plain flour
pinch of salt
7.5ml/1½ tsp easy-blend dried yeast
25g/1oz/2 tbsp soft light
  brown sugar
2 eggs, beaten
45ml/3 tbsp warm milk
crème fraîche, to serve

For the syrup

115g/4oz/generous ½ cup
  granulated sugar
120ml/4fl oz/½ cup water
450g/1lb plums, halved, stoned and
  thickly sliced
120ml/4fl oz/½ cup brewed coffee
45ml/3 tbsp dark rum

4 Cover with clear film and leave to rise for 40 minutes. Cut the remaining butter into cubes and mix into the dough. Put the tins on a baking tray and drop the dough into the moulds. Cover with oiled clear film and leave until the dough has almost risen to the top. Remove the film and bake for 15–20 minutes.

5 Meanwhile make the syrup. Put 25g/1oz/2 tbsp of the sugar in a pan with the water. Add the plums and cook over a low heat until barely tender; remove with a slotted spoon. Add the remaining sugar and coffee to the pan. Heat gently until dissolved, but do not boil. Remove from the heat and stir in the rum.

6 Turn out the babas on to a wire rack and leave to cool for 5 minutes. Dunk them in the warm syrup until well soaked. Return them to the wire rack with a plate underneath to catch any drips. Leave to cool completely.

7 Put the babas on a serving plate and fill the middles with the sliced plums. Spoon a little extra syrup over each and serve with crème fraîche.

1 Preheat the oven to 190°C/375°F/Gas 5. Thickly brush six 9cm/3½in ring tins with 15g/½oz/1 tbsp of the butter.

2 Sift the flour and salt into a mixing bowl and stir in the yeast and soft light brown sugar.

3 Make a well in the middle and add the eggs and warm milk. Beat for about 5 minutes with a wooden spoon to make a very sticky dough that is fairly smooth and elastic.

COOK'S TIP

The babas may also be split in half horizontally, filled with whipped cream and sandwiched back together.

COCONUT AND COFFEE TRIFLE

Dark coffee sponge, laced with liqueur, coconut custard and a coffee cream topping makes this a lavish dessert. Serve in a large glass bowl for maximum impact.

SERVES SIX TO EIGHT

INGREDIENTS

For the coffee sponge
   45ml/3 tbsp strong-flavoured
      ground coffee
   45ml/3 tbsp near-boiling water
   2 eggs
   50g/2oz/¼ cup soft dark brown sugar
   40g/1½oz/⅓ cup self-raising
      flour, sifted
   25ml/1½ tbsp hazelnut or
      sunflower oil
For the coconut custard
   400ml/14fl oz/1⅔ cup canned
      coconut milk
   3 eggs
   40g/1½oz/3 tbsp caster sugar
   10ml/2 tsp cornflour
For the filling and topping
   2 medium bananas
   60ml/4 tbsp coffee liqueur, such as
      Tia Maria, Kahlúa or Toussaint
   300ml/½ pint/1¼ cups double cream
   30ml/2 tbsp icing sugar, sifted
   ribbons of fresh coconut, to decorate

1 Preheat the oven to 160°C/325°F/ Gas 3. Grease and line an 18cm/7in square tin with greaseproof paper.

2 Put the coffee in a small bowl. Pour the hot water over and leave to infuse for 4 minutes. Strain through a fine sieve, discarding the grounds.

3 Whisk the eggs and soft dark brown sugar in a large bowl until the whisk leaves a trail when lifted.

4 Gently fold in the flour, followed by 15ml/1 tbsp of the coffee and the oil. Spoon the mixture into the tin and bake for 20 minutes, until firm. Turn out on to a wire rack, remove the lining paper and leave to cool.

5 To make the coconut custard, heat the coconut milk in a saucepan until it is almost boiling.

6 Whisk the eggs, sugar and cornflour together until frothy. Pour on the hot coconut milk, whisking all the time. Add to the pan and heat gently, stirring for 1–2 minutes, until the custard thickens, but do not boil. Set aside to cool for about 10 minutes, stirring occasionally.

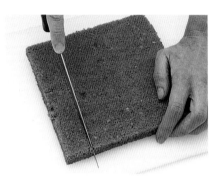

7 Cut the coffee sponge into 5cm/2in squares and arrange in the base of a large glass bowl. Slice the bananas and arrange on top of the sponge. Drizzle the coffee liqueur on top. Pour the custard over and leave until cold.

8 Whip the cream with the remaining coffee and icing sugar until soft peaks form. Spoon the cream over the custard. Cover and chill for several hours. Sprinkle with ribbons of fresh coconut before serving.

COOK'S TIP
To make coconut ribbons, use a vegetable peeler to cut thin ribbons from the flesh of a fresh coconut, or buy shredded coconut and toast until it is pale golden.

FLAMBÉED BANANAS <u>WITH</u> CARIBBEAN COFFEE SAUCE

THIS DESSERT HAS ALL THE FLAVOUR OF THE CARIBBEAN; BANANAS, DARK SUGAR, COFFEE AND RUM.

SERVES FOUR TO SIX

INGREDIENTS
 6 bananas
 40g/1½oz/3 tbsp butter
 50g/2oz/¼ cup soft dark brown sugar
 50ml/2fl oz/¼ cup strong
  brewed coffee
 60ml/4 tbsp dark rum
 vanilla ice cream, to serve

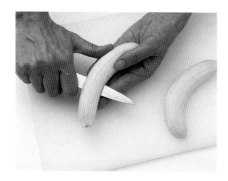

1 Peel the bananas and cut in half lengthways. Melt the butter in a large frying pan over a medium heat. Add the bananas and cook for 3 minutes, turning halfway through cooking time.

COOK'S TIP
These hot bananas taste equally good served with coconut or coffee ice cream.

2 Sprinkle the sugar over the bananas, then add the coffee. Continue cooking, stirring occasionally, for 2–3 minutes, or until the bananas are tender.

3 Pour the rum into the pan and bring to the boil. With a long match or taper and tilting the pan, ignite the rum. As soon as the flames subside, serve the bananas with vanilla ice cream.

GRILLED NECTARINES <u>WITH</u> COFFEE MASCARPONE FILLING

THIS SIMPLE DESSERT IS PERFECT FOR NECTARINES THAT ARE STILL SLIGHTLY HARD, AS THEY'RE GRILLED WITH A DELICIOUS HONEY AND BUTTER GLAZE AND FILLED WITH CHILLED COFFEE CREAM.

SERVES FOUR

INGREDIENTS
 115g/4oz/½ cup mascarpone
 45ml/3 tbsp cold very strong
  brewed coffee
 4 nectarines
 15g/½oz/1 tbsp butter, melted
  and cooled
 45ml/3 tbsp clear honey
 pinch of ground mixed spice
 25g/1oz/¼ cup slivered brazil nuts

1 Beat the mascarpone until softened, then gradually mix in the cold brewed coffee. Cover with clear film and chill for 20 minutes.

2 Cut the nectarines in half and remove the stones. In a small bowl, mix the butter, 30ml/2 tbsp of the honey and ground mixed spice. Brush the spicy butter all over the cut surfaces.

3 Arrange the nectarines, cut-side up on a foil-lined grill pan. Cook under a hot grill for 2–3 minutes. Add the brazil nuts to the grill pan for the last minute of cooking and toast until golden.

4 Put a spoonful of the chilled cheese mixture in the centre of each hot nectarine. Drizzle with the remaining honey and sprinkle with the toasted brazil nuts before serving.

COOK'S TIP
If possible, choose a scented honey for this dessert: orange blossom and rosemary are both delicious.

CARAMELIZED APPLES

A TRADITIONAL DESSERT WITH A DIFFERENCE — BAKED APPLES BATHED IN A RICH COFFEE SYRUP.

SERVES SIX

INGREDIENTS

6 eating apples, peeled, but
  left whole
50g/2oz/4 tbsp unsalted butter,
  melted and cooled
90g/3½oz/½ cup caster sugar
1.5ml/¼ tsp ground cinnamon
90ml/6 tbsp strong brewed coffee
whipped or clotted cream,
  to serve

COOK'S TIP
This recipe is equally good made with
pears, but reduce the cooking time by
10–15 minutes and use mixed spice in
place of the cinnamon.

1 Preheat the oven to 180°C/350°F/
Gas 4. Cut a thin slice from the bottom
of each apple to give them a flat base.
Using a pastry brush, thickly coat each
apple with melted butter.

2 Mix the caster sugar and cinnamon
in a shallow dish. Holding each apple
by its stalk, roll in the mixture to coat.

3 Arrange the apples in a shallow
baking dish into which they just fit.
Stand them upright.

4 Pour the coffee into the dish then
sprinkle over any remaining sugar
mixture. Bake the apples for 40 minutes,
basting with the coffee two or three
times throughout. Baste a last time,
then pour the juices into a small pan,
returning the apples to the oven.

5 Boil the juices rapidly until syrupy
and reduced to about 60ml/4 tbsp. Pour
over the apples and cook for 10 more
minutes, or until the apples are tender.
Serve hot with a spoonful of cream.

SUMMER BERRIES <u>WITH</u> COFFEE SABAYON

*FOR A LIGHT AND DELICIOUSLY REFRESHING FINALE, SERVE A PLATTER OF FRESH SUMMER FRUIT WITH
A FLUFFY COFFEE SAUCE, WHICH HAS THE ADDED ADVANTAGE OF BEING DELIGHTFULLY EASY TO MAKE.*

SERVES SIX

INGREDIENTS

900g/2lb/6–8 cups mixed summer
  berries such as raspberries,
  blueberries and strawberries (hulled
  and halved, if large)
5 egg yolks
75g/3oz/scant ½ cup caster sugar
50ml/2fl oz/¼ cup brewed coffee
30ml/2 tbsp coffee liqueur, such as
  Tia Maria, Kahlúa or Toussaint
strawberry or mint leaves,
  to decorate (optional)
30ml/2 tbsp icing sugar, to dust

COOK'S TIP
Ensure that the water doesn't get too hot
when making the sauce, or it may curdle.

1 Arrange the fruit on a serving platter
and decorate with strawberry or mint
leaves, if you like. Dust with icing sugar.

2 Whisk the egg yolks and caster sugar
in a bowl over a pan of simmering water
until the mixture begins to thicken.

3 Gradually add the coffee and liqueur,
pouring in a thin, continuous stream
and whisking all the time. Continue
whisking until the sauce is thick and
fluffy. Serve warm, or allow to cool,
whisking occasionally, and serve cold
with the fruit.

FROZEN DESSERTS

Frozen desserts are an ideal choice for all occasions as they can be made in advance, then stored in the freezer. In this chapter, you'll find smooth, velvety ice cream and refreshing sorbets. Some ices are only part of the dessert, such as in Dark Chocolate and Coffee Mousse Cake, a rich chocolate sponge with an ice cream centre.

CINNAMON <u>AND</u> COFFEE SWIRL ICE CREAM

LIGHT ICE CREAM SUBTLY SPICED WITH CINNAMON AND RIPPLED WITH A SWEET COFFEE SYRUP.

SERVES SIX

INGREDIENTS
    300ml/½ pint/1¼ cups single cream
    1 cinnamon stick
    4 egg yolks
    150g/5oz/¾ cup caster sugar
    300ml/½ pint/1¼ cups
      double cream
For the coffee syrup
    45ml/3 tbsp ground coffee
    45ml/3 tbsp near-boiling water
    90g/3½oz/½ cup caster sugar
    50ml/2fl oz/¼ cup water

1 Pour the single cream into a small pan and add the cinnamon stick. Slowly bring to the boil. Turn off the heat, cover with a lid and leave to infuse for 30 minutes. Bring back to the boil and remove the cinnamon stick.

2 Whisk the yolks and sugar until light. Pour the hot cream over the egg mixture, whisking. Return to the pan and stir over low heat for 1–2 minutes, until it thickens. Allow to cool.

3 Whip the double cream until peaks form and fold into the custard. Pour into a container and freeze for 3 hours.

4 Meanwhile, to make the syrup, put the coffee in a bowl and pour the hot water over. Leave to infuse for 4 minutes, then strain through a sieve.

COOK'S TIP
Make sure that the cinnamon ice cream is sufficiently frozen before adding the coffee syrup.

5 Gently heat the sugar and cold water in a pan until completely dissolved. Bring to the boil and gently simmer for 5 minutes. Cool, then stir in the coffee.

6 Turn the cinnamon ice cream into a chilled bowl and briefly whisk to break down the ice crystals.

7 Spoon a third back into the container and drizzle some of the coffee syrup over. Repeat in this way until all is used.

8 Drag a skewer through the mixture a few times to achieve a marbled effect. Freeze for 4 hours, or until solid. Allow to soften slightly before serving.

TOASTED NUT AND COFFEE ICE CREAM IN BRANDY SNAP BASKETS

SCOOPS OF CRUSHED CARAMEL AND TOASTED NUT ICE CREAM ARE SERVED IN CRISP CASES, THEN DRIZZLED WITH A WARM COFFEE AND COGNAC SAUCE.

SERVES SIX

INGREDIENTS
75g/3oz/½ cup whole nuts, such as
  blanched almonds and hazelnuts
90g/3½oz/½ cup caster sugar
1 vanilla pod, split
30ml/2 tbsp ground coffee
200ml/7fl oz/scant 1 cup
  double cream
300ml/½ pint/1¼ cups Greek yogurt
6 brandy snap baskets, to serve
For the coffee and cognac sauce
115g/4oz/½ cup soft light
  brown sugar
50ml/2fl oz/¼ cup hot water
100ml/3½fl oz/½ cup strong
  brewed coffee
60ml/4 tbsp cognac

2 Pour on to an oiled baking sheet to cool and harden. Crush to a fine powder. Put the vanilla, coffee and cream in a pan. Heat almost to boiling, turn off the heat, cover and infuse.

3 After 15 minutes, strain through a sieve and leave to cool. Stir the coffee cream into the yogurt with the crushed nut mixture. Transfer to a freezerproof container and freeze for 4 hours.

4 To make the sauce, heat the sugar and water in a small heavy-based pan over a gentle heat until melted. Simmer for 3 minutes. Cool slightly, then stir in the coffee and cognac.

5 Meanwhile, allow the ice cream to soften in the fridge for 15 minutes. Scoop into the brandy snap baskets and serve immediately with the warm coffee and cognac sauce.

1 Put the whole nuts and caster sugar in a large heavy-based pan and heat gently until the sugar caramelizes to a light golden brown, shaking the pan only occasionally.

COOK'S TIP
To make brandy snap baskets, in a bowl, gently melt 50g/2oz/4 tbsp butter, 50g/2oz/¼ cup demerara sugar and 50g/2oz/¼ cup golden syrup. Stir in 50g/2oz/½ cup sifted plain flour and 5ml/1 tsp brandy. Drop well-spaced teaspoons on to oiled baking trays. Bake in a preheated oven at 160°C/325°F/Gas 3 for about 8 minutes. Cool for 1 minute, then lift with a palette knife and mould over the base of an inverted glass.

COFFEE ICE CREAM

FRESHLY GROUND COFFEE GIVES THIS CLASSIC ICE CREAM A DISTINCTIVE AND SOPHISTICATED FLAVOUR. CHOOSE A DARK-ROASTED BEAN TO ENSURE A RICH, GLOSSY COLOUR TO THE ICE CREAM.

SERVES EIGHT TO TEN

INGREDIENTS
   60ml/4 tbsp dark-roasted
      ground coffee
   600ml/1 pint/2½ cups milk
   200g/7oz/scant 1 cup soft light
      brown sugar
   6 egg yolks
   475ml/16fl oz/2 cups
      whipping cream

1 Put the coffee in a jug. Heat the milk in a saucepan to near-boiling point and pour over the coffee. Leave to stand for 4 minutes.

2 Meanwhile, in a large bowl, beat the sugar and egg yolks until light. Pour the milk over, whisking all the time. Strain the mixture back into the pan through a fine sieve.

3 Cook the custard over a low heat for 1–2 minutes, stirring until it coats the back of a wooden spoon. Do not boil. Pour into a shallow freezer container and leave to cool, stirring occasionally.

COOK'S TIP
If using an ice cream maker, do not whip the cream: stir it into the coffee custard before adding to the machine.

4 Freeze for about 2 hours, then tip into a bowl and whisk with a fork until smooth. Whip the cream until peaks form and fold into the frozen mixture.

5 Return to the freezer for 1 more hour, then turn out and whisk again. Finally, freeze for 3–4 hours, until solid. Transfer to the fridge for 20 minutes, before scooping and serving.

CAPPUCCINO CONES

PRETTY WHITE AND DARK CHOCOLATE CONES ARE FILLED WITH SWIRLS OF CAPPUCCINO CREAM AND TOPPED WITH A LIGHT DUSTING OF COCOA POWDER.

SERVES SIX

INGREDIENTS
   115g/4oz each good quality plain and
      white cooking chocolate
For the cappuccino cream
   30ml/2 tbsp ground espresso or other
      strong-flavoured coffee
   30ml/2 tbsp near-boiling water
   300ml/½ pint/1¼ cups double cream
   45ml/3 tbsp icing sugar, sifted
   15ml/1 tbsp cocoa powder,
      for dusting

1 Cut nine 13 x 10cm/5 x 4in rectangles from non-stick baking parchment, then cut each rectangle in half diagonally to make 18 triangles. Roll up each to make a cone and secure with sticky tape.

2 Heat the plain chocolate in a bowl over a pan of hot water until melted. Using a small pastry brush, thickly brush the insides of half the paper cones with chocolate. Chill until set. Repeat with the white chocolate. Carefully peel away the paper and keep the cones in the fridge until needed.

3 To make the cappuccino cream, put the coffee in a small bowl. Pour the hot water over. Leave to infuse for 4 minutes, then strain though a fine sieve into a bowl. Leave to cool. Add the cream and sugar and whisk until soft peaks form. Spoon into an icing bag fitted with a medium star nozzle.

4 Pipe the cream into the chocolate cones. Put on a baking sheet and freeze for at least 2 hours or until solid. Arrange on individual plates, allowing three cones per person and dusting with cocoa powder before serving.

COOK'S TIP
Make sure, when melting the chocolate, that the water doesn't boil or the chocolate will overheat and stiffen.

MAPLE COFFEE AND PISTACHIO BOMBES

REAL MAPLE SYRUP TASTES INFINITELY BETTER THAN THE SYNTHETIC VARIETIES AND IS WELL WORTH SEARCHING FOR. HERE IT SWEETENS THE DARK COFFEE CENTRE OF THESE PRETTY PISTACHIO BOMBES.

<u>SERVES SIX</u>

INGREDIENTS

For the pistachio ice cream
   50g/2oz/¼ cup caster sugar
   50ml/2fl oz/¼ cup water
   175g/6oz can evaporated
    milk, chilled
   50g/2oz/½ cup shelled and skinned
    pistachio nuts, finely chopped
   drop of green food colouring
    (optional)
   200ml/7fl oz/scant 1 cup
    whipping cream
For the maple coffee centres
   30ml/2 tbsp ground coffee
   150ml/¼ pint/⅔ cup single cream
   50ml/2fl oz/¼ cup maple syrup
   2 egg yolks
   5ml/1 tsp cornflour
   150ml/¼ pint/⅔ cup whipping cream

1 Put six 175ml/6fl oz/¾ cup mini pudding basins or dariole moulds into the freezer to chill. Put the sugar and water in a heavy-based saucepan and heat gently until dissolved. Bring to the boil and simmer for 3 minutes.

2 Cool, then stir in the chilled evaporated milk, pistachio nuts and colouring, if using. Lightly whip the cream until it forms soft peaks and blend into the mixture.

3 Pour the mixture into a freezerproof container and freeze for at least 2 hours. Whisk the ice cream until smooth, then freeze for a further 2 hours or until frozen, but not solid.

4 To make the centres, put the ground coffee in a jug. Heat the single cream to near-boiling point and pour over the coffee. Leave to infuse for 4 minutes. Whisk the maple syrup, egg yolks and cornflour together. Strain the hot coffee cream over the egg mixture, whisking continuously. Return to the pan and cook gently for 1–2 minutes, until the custard thickens. Leave to cool, stirring occasionally.

5 Meanwhile, line the moulds with the ice cream, keeping the thickness as even as possible right up to the rim. Freeze until the ice cream is firm again.

6 Beat the cream until peaks form, then fold into the custard. Spoon into the middle of the moulds. Cover and freeze for 2 hours. Serve immediately.

FROSTED RASPBERRY AND COFFEE TERRINE

A WHITE CHOCOLATE AND RASPBERRY LAYER AND A CONTRASTING SMOOTH COFFEE LAYER MAKE THIS ATTRACTIVE LOOKING DESSERT DOUBLY DELICIOUS.

SERVES SIX TO EIGHT

INGREDIENTS
  30ml/2 tbsp ground coffee,
    e.g. mocha orange-flavoured
  250ml/8fl oz/1 cup milk
  4 eggs, separated
  50g/2oz/¼ cup caster sugar
  30ml/2 tbsp cornflour
  150ml/¼ pint/⅔ cup double cream
  150g/5oz white chocolate,
    roughly chopped
  115g/4oz/⅔ cup raspberries
  shavings of white chocolate and
    cocoa powder, to decorate

1 Line a 1.5 litre/2½ pint/6¼ cup loaf tin with clear film and put in the freezer to chill. Put the ground coffee in a jug. Heat 100ml/3½fl oz/scant ½ cup of the milk to near-boiling point and pour over the coffee. Leave to infuse.

2 Blend the egg yolks, sugar and cornflour together in a saucepan and whisk in the remaining milk and the cream. Bring to the boil, stirring all the time, until thickened.

3 Divide the hot mixture between two bowls and add the white chocolate to one, stirring until melted. Strain the coffee through a fine sieve into the other bowl and mix well. Leave until cool, stirring occasionally.

COOK'S TIP
After decorating, allow the terrine to soften in the fridge for 20 minutes before slicing and serving.

4 Whisk two of the egg whites until stiff. Fold into the coffee custard. Spoon into the tin and freeze for 30 minutes. Whisk remaining whites and fold into the chocolate mixture with the raspberries.

5 Spoon into the tin and level before freezing for 4 hours. Turn the terrine out on to a flat serving plate and peel off the clear film. Cover with chocolate shavings and dust with cocoa powder.

COFFEE AND MINTY-LEMON SORBET

THE FLAVOURS OF FRESH MINT, SHARP LEMON AND AROMATIC COFFEE ARE COMBINED IN THIS DELICIOUS ICY SORBET. THE LEMON SHELLS ARE AN EASY, BUT PRETTY, SUMMERY DECORATIVE TOUCH.

SERVES SIX

INGREDIENTS
115g/4oz/generous ½ cup sugar
400ml/14fl oz/1⅔ cups water
15g/½oz fresh mint leaves
30ml/2 tbsp coffee liqueur, such as
  Tia Maria, Kahlúa or Toussaint
6 lemons
1 egg white
sprigs of fresh mint, to decorate

1 Put the sugar in a large heavy-based saucepan with the water and heat gently until dissolved, stirring occasionally. Bring to the boil, and simmer for 5 minutes.

COOK'S TIP
Fresh fruit sorbets will keep in the freezer for up to 2 months, but are best eaten within several days of making.

2 Remove from the heat, add the mint leaves, stir and leave to cool. Strain into a jug and stir in the liqueur.

3 Cut a thin slice from the base of each lemon so that they will stand upright, being careful not to cut through the pith. Cut the tops off the lemons and keep for lids. Scrape out the lemon flesh and squeeze the juice. Strain the juice into the mint and coffee syrup.

4 Pour into a freezerproof container and freeze for 3 hours. Whisk to break down the ice crystals, then freeze for 1 more hour. Whisk the egg white until stiff, then whisk into the ice. Scoop into the lemon shells and replace the lids.

5 Place upright on a tray and freeze for 2 hours, until solid. Transfer to the fridge 5 minutes before serving, to soften. Decorate with sprigs of mint.

ESPRESSO GRANITA

THIS FAMOUS FROZEN ITALIAN ICE MAKES A REFRESHING FINISH TO A RICH MEAL.

SERVES SIX

INGREDIENTS
90g/3½oz/½ cup sugar
600ml/1 pint/2½ cups espresso or
  other strong-flavoured coffee
whipped cream, to serve
  (optional)

COOK'S TIPS
• Don't whisk the granita too vigorously – it should have a rough granular texture, rather than a smooth one like a sorbet.
• After step 3, the granita can either be served at that stage or covered and stored in the freezer for up to 2 weeks.

1 Add the sugar to the hot coffee and stir until dissolved. Leave to cool, then pour into a 900ml/1½ pint/3¾ cup shallow freezer container.

2 Freeze for at least 3 hours, or until ice crystals form around the edges. Whisk with a fork, then return to the freezer for another hour.

3 Whisk the mixture again with a fork and re-freeze. Repeat until the mixture is frozen and there is no liquid.

4 Transfer the granita to the fridge 20 minutes before serving. Break up the ice crystals with a strong fork and serve in glasses, topped with whipped cream, if you like.

ICED COFFEE MOUSSE <u>IN A</u> CHOCOLATE CASE

A DARK CHOCOLATE BOWL IS FILLED WITH A LIGHT, ICED COFFEE MOUSSE. IT LOOKS A DRAMATIC DESSERT, BUT ISN'T DIFFICULT TO MAKE.

SERVES EIGHT

INGREDIENTS
   1 sachet powdered gelatine
   60ml/4 tbsp very strong
      brewed coffee
   30ml/2 tbsp coffee liqueur, such as
      Tia Maria, Kahlúa or Toussaint
   3 eggs, separated
   75g/3oz/scant ½ cup caster sugar
   150ml/¼ pint/⅔ cup whipping cream,
      lightly whipped
For the chocolate bowl
   225g/8oz plain chocolate squares,
      plus extra for decoration

1 Grease and line a deep 18cm/7in loose-based cake tin with non-stick baking parchment.

2 Melt the chocolate in a bowl over a pan of simmering water. Using a pastry brush, brush a layer of chocolate over the base of the tin and about 7.5cm/3in up the sides, finishing with a ragged edge. Allow the chocolate to set before repeating. Put in the freezer to harden.

3 Sprinkle the gelatine over the coffee in a bowl and leave to soften for 5 minutes. Put the bowl over a pan of simmering water, stirring until dissolved. Remove from the heat and stir in the liqueur. Whisk the egg yolks and sugar in a bowl over the simmering water until thick enough to leave a trail. Remove from the pan and whisk until cool. Whisk the egg whites until stiff.

4 Pour the dissolved gelatine into the egg yolk mixture in a thin stream, stirring gently. Chill in the fridge for 20 minutes, or until just beginning to set, then fold in the cream, followed by the whisked egg whites.

5 Remove the chocolate case from the freezer and peel away the lining. Put it back in the tin, then pour in the mousse. Return to the freezer for at least 3 hours. To serve, remove from the tin and place on a plate. Allow to soften in the fridge for 40 minutes before serving. Decorate with grated chocolate. Use a knife dipped in hot water and wiped dry to cut into slices to serve.

DARK CHOCOLATE <u>AND</u> COFFEE MOUSSE CAKE

THIS DOUBLE TREAT WILL PROVE IRRESISTIBLE — RICH SPONGE FILLED WITH CREAMY COFFEE MOUSSE.

SERVES EIGHT

INGREDIENTS
    4 eggs
    115g/4oz/generous ½ cup
        caster sugar
    75g/3oz/⅔ cup plain flour, sifted
    25g/1oz/¼ cup cocoa powder, sifted
    60ml/4 tbsp coffee liqueur, such as
        Tia Maria, Kahlúa or Toussaint
    icing sugar, to dust
For the coffee mousse
    30ml/2 tbsp dark-roasted
        ground coffee beans
    350ml/12fl oz/1½ cups double cream
    115g/4oz/generous ½ cup
        granulated sugar
    120ml/4fl oz/½ cup water
    4 egg yolks

1 Preheat the oven to 180°C/350°F/ Gas 4. Grease and line the bases of a 20cm/8in square and a 23cm/9in round cake tin with non-stick baking parchment. Put the eggs and sugar in a bowl over a pan of hot water and whisk until thick.

2 Remove from the heat and whisk until thick enough to leave a trail when the whisk is lifted. Gently fold in the flour and cocoa. Pour a third of the mixture into the square tin and the remainder into the round tin. Bake the square sponge for 15 minutes and the round for 30 minutes, until firm.

3 Cool on a wire rack before slicing the round cake in half horizontally. Place the bottom half back in the tin. Sprinkle with half the liqueur.

4 Trim the edges of the square sponge, cut into 4 equal strips and use to line the sides of the tin.

5 To make the mousse, put the coffee in a bowl. Heat 50ml/2fl oz/¼ cup of the cream to near-boiling and pour over the coffee. Leave to infuse for 4 minutes, then strain through a fine sieve.

6 Gently heat the sugar and water until dissolved. Increase the heat and boil steadily until the syrup reaches 107°C/ 225°F. Cool for 5 minutes, then pour on to the egg yolks, whisking until the mixture is very thick.

7 Add the coffee cream to the remaining cream and whip until soft peaks form. Fold into the egg mixture. Spoon into the sponge case and freeze for 20 minutes. Sprinkle the remaining liqueur over the second sponge half and place on top of the mousse. Cover and freeze for 4 hours. Remove from the tin and dust with icing sugar.

COOK'S TIP
Cover the seams of the cake with swirls of piped whipped cream and decorate with chocolate coffee beans, if you like.

CAKES AND TORTES

From simple sponges to elaborate

tortes and velvety cheesecakes, these

are cakes to rival any shop-bought

confection. Some, such as Coffee

Almond Marsala Slice, are perfect

with mid-morning coffee. Others,

like Coffee Chocolate Mousse Cake

and Cappuccino Torte, make

unforgettable dinner party desserts.

COCONUT COFFEE CAKE

COCONUT AND COFFEE ARE NATURAL PARTNERS, AS THESE LITTLE SQUARES OF ICED CAKE PROVE.

SERVES NINE

INGREDIENTS
   45ml/3 tbsp ground coffee
   75ml/5 tbsp near-boiling milk
   25g/1oz/2 tbsp caster sugar
   175g/6oz/²⁄₃ cup golden syrup
   75g/3oz/6 tbsp butter
   40g/1½oz/½ cup desiccated coconut
   175g/6oz/1½ cups plain flour
   2.5ml/½ tsp bicarbonate of soda
   2 eggs, lightly beaten
For the icing
   115g/4oz/8 tbsp butter, softened
   225g/8oz/2 cups icing sugar, sifted
   25g/1oz/⅓ cup shredded or flaked
     coconut, toasted

1 Preheat the oven to 160°C/325°F/ Gas 3. Grease and line the base of a 20cm/8in square tin.

2 Put the ground coffee in a small bowl and pour the hot milk over. Leave to infuse for 4 minutes, then strain through a fine sieve.

3 Heat the caster sugar, golden syrup, butter and desiccated coconut in a pan, stirring with a wooden spoon, until completely melted.

4 Sift the flour and bicarbonate of soda together and stir into the mixture, along with the eggs and 45ml/3 tbsp of the coffee-flavoured milk.

5 Spoon the mixture into the prepared tin and level the top. Bake in the oven for 40–50 minutes until well-risen and firm. Allow the cake to cool in the tin for about 10 minutes, before running a knife around the edges to loosen. Turn out and cool on a wire rack.

6 To make the icing, beat the softened butter until smooth then gradually beat in the icing sugar and remaining coffee milk to give a soft consistency. Spread over the top of the cake and decorate with toasted coconut. Cut into 5cm/2in squares to serve.

VARIATION
Substitute 50g/2oz/½ cup chopped pecan nuts for the desiccated coconut and decorate the squares with pecan halves dusted with icing sugar.

MOCHA SPONGE CAKE

THE YEMENI CITY OF MOCHA WAS ONCE CONSIDERED TO BE THE COFFEE CAPITAL OF THE WORLD, AND STILL PRODUCES A COFFEE THAT TASTES A LITTLE LIKE CHOCOLATE. TODAY "MOCHA" MAY REFER TO THE VARIETY OF COFFEE OR MEAN A COMBINATION OF COFFEE OR CHOCOLATE, AS IN THIS RECIPE.

SERVES TEN

INGREDIENTS

    25ml/1½ tbsp strong-flavoured
      ground coffee
    175ml/6fl oz/¾ cup milk
    115g/4oz/8 tbsp butter
    115g/4oz/½ cup soft light
      brown sugar
    1 egg, lightly beaten
    185g/6½oz/1⅔ cups self-raising flour
    5ml/1 tsp bicarbonate of soda
    60ml/4 tbsp creamy liqueur, such as
      Baileys or Irish Velvet
For the glossy chocolate icing
    200g/7oz plain chocolate, broken
      into pieces
    75g/3oz/6 tbsp unsalted
      butter, cubed
    120ml/4fl oz/½ cup double cream

1 Preheat the oven to 180°C/350°F/
Gas 4. Grease and line a 18cm/7in
round fixed-base cake tin with
greaseproof paper.

2 To make the cake, put the coffee in
a jug. Heat the milk to near-boiling and
pour over. Leave to infuse for 4 minutes,
then strain through a sieve and cool.

3 Gently melt the butter and sugar until
dissolved. Pour into a bowl and cool for
2 minutes, then stir in the egg.

4 Sift the flour over the mixture and
fold in. Blend the bicarbonate of soda
with the coffee-flavoured milk and
gradually stir into the mixture.

5 Pour into the tin, smooth the surface,
and bake for 40 minutes, until well-
risen and firm. Cool in the tin for about
10 minutes. Spoon the liqueur over the
cake and leave until cold. Loosen the
edges with a palette knife and turn out
on to a wire rack.

6 To make the icing, place the broken
chocolate in a bowl over a pan of barely
simmering water until melted. Remove
from the heat and stir in the butter and
cream until smooth. Allow to cool before
coating the top and sides of the cake,
using a palette knife. Leave until set.

COFFEE ALMOND MARSALA SLICE

ROASTED AND CRUSHED COFFEE BEANS ARE SPECKLED THROUGHOUT THIS DELICIOUS ALMOND CAKE, DISTINCTLY FLAVOURED WITH ITALIAN MARSALA WINE.

SERVES TEN TO TWELVE

INGREDIENTS
  25g/1oz/⅓ cup roasted coffee beans
  5 eggs, separated
  175g/6oz/scant 1 cup caster sugar
  120ml/4fl oz/½ cup Marsala wine
  75g/3oz/6 tbsp butter, melted
    and cooled
  115g/4oz/1 cup ground almonds
  115g/4oz/1 cup plain flour, sifted
  25g/1oz/¼ cup flaked almonds
  icing sugar, to dust
  crème fraîche, to serve

1 Preheat the oven to 180°C/350°F/
Gas 4. Grease and line the base of a
23cm/9in round loose-based tin with
greaseproof paper. Put the coffee beans
on a baking sheet and roast for about
10 minutes. Cool, then place in a large
plastic bag and gently crush with a
rolling pin.

2 Beat the yolks and 115g/4oz/
generous ½ cup of the caster sugar
until very pale and thick.

3 Stir in the crushed coffee, Marsala,
butter and almonds. Sift the flour over,
then carefully fold in.

4 Whisk the egg whites until they are
stiff, then gradually incorporate the
remaining caster sugar.

5 Fold into the almond mixture, a third
at a time. Spoon into the tin and
sprinkle the top with flaked almonds.

6 Bake for 10 minutes, then reduce
the oven to 160°C/325°F/Gas 3 and
cook for a further 40 minutes, or until
a skewer inserted into the centre comes
out clean. After 5 minutes, turn out and
cool on a wire rack. Dust with icing
sugar and serve with crème fraîche.

SOUR CHERRY COFFEE LOAF

DRIED SOUR CHERRIES HAVE A WONDERFULLY CONCENTRATED FRUIT FLAVOUR AND CAN BE BOUGHT IN SUPERMARKETS AND HEALTH FOOD SHOPS.

SERVES EIGHT

INGREDIENTS
  175g/6oz/12 tbsp butter, softened
  175g/6oz/scant 1 cup golden
    caster sugar
  5ml/1 tsp vanilla extract
  2 eggs, lightly beaten
  225g/8oz/2 cups plain flour
  1.5ml/¼ tsp baking powder
  75ml/5 tbsp strong brewed coffee
  175g/6oz/1 cup dried sour cherries
For the icing
  50g/2oz/½ cup icing sugar, sifted
  20ml/4 tsp strong brewed coffee

1 Preheat the oven to 180°C/350°F/
Gas 4. Grease and line a 900g/2lb loaf
tin with greaseproof paper. Cream the
butter, sugar and vanilla until fluffy.

2 Gradually add the eggs, beating well
after each addition. Sift the flour and
baking powder together.

3 Fold into the mixture with the coffee
and 115g/4oz/⅔ cup of the sour
cherries. Spoon the mixture into the
prepared tin and level the top.

4 Bake for 1¼ hours or until firm to the
touch. Cool in the tin for 5 minutes,
then turn out and cool on a wire rack.

5 To make the icing, mix together the
icing sugar and coffee and the
remaining cherries. Spoon over the top
and sides. Leave to set before slicing.

COFFEE AND MINT CREAM CAKE

GROUND ALMONDS GIVE THIS BUTTERY COFFEE SPONGE A MOIST TEXTURE AND DELICATE FLAVOUR. IT'S SANDWICHED TOGETHER WITH A GENEROUS FILLING OF CRÈME DE MENTHE BUTTERCREAM.

SERVES EIGHT

INGREDIENTS

    15ml/1 tbsp ground coffee
    25ml/1½ tbsp near-boiling water
    175g/6oz/12 tbsp unsalted
      butter, softened
    175g/6oz/scant 1 cup
      caster sugar
    225g/8oz/2 cups self-raising
      flour, sifted
    50g/2oz/½ cup ground almonds
    3 eggs
    small sprigs of fresh mint,
      to decorate
For the filling
    50g/2oz/4 tbsp unsalted butter
    115g/4oz/1 cup icing sugar, sifted,
      plus extra for dusting
    30ml/2 tbsp crème de
      menthe liqueur

1 Preheat the oven to 180°C/350°F/ Gas 4. Lightly grease and base line two 18cm/7in sandwich tins with greaseproof paper.

2 Put the coffee in a bowl and pour the hot water over. Leave to infuse for about 4 minutes, then strain through a sieve.

3 Put the butter, sugar, flour, almonds, eggs and coffee in a large bowl. Beat well for 1 minute until blended. Divide the mixture evenly between the tins and level off. Bake for 25 minutes until well-risen and firm to the touch. Leave in the tins for 5 minutes, then turn out on to a wire rack to cool.

4 To make the filling, cream the unsalted butter, icing sugar and crème de menthe liqueur together in a bowl until light and fluffy.

COOK'S TIP
Make sure the butter is really soft and creamy before starting to mix the cake.

5 Remove the lining paper from the sponges and sandwich together with the filling.

6 Generously dust the top with icing sugar and place on a serving plate. Scatter with the fresh mint leaves just before serving.

COFFEE AND WALNUT SWISS ROLL WITH COINTREAU CREAM

COFFEE AND WALNUTS HAVE A NATURAL AFFINITY. HERE THEY APPEAR TOGETHER IN A LIGHT AND FLUFFY SPONGE ENCLOSING A SMOOTH ORANGE CREAM.

SERVES SIX

INGREDIENTS

    10ml/2 tsp ground coffee,
      e.g. mocha orange-flavoured
    15ml/1 tbsp near-boiling water
    3 eggs
    75g/3oz/scant ½ cup caster sugar,
      plus extra for dusting
    75g/3oz/⅔ cup self-raising flour
    50g/2oz/½ cup toasted walnuts,
      finely chopped
For the Cointreau cream
    115g/4oz/generous ½ cup
      caster sugar
    50ml/2fl oz/¼ cup cold water
    2 egg yolks
    115g/4oz/8 tbsp unsalted
      butter, softened
    15ml/1 tbsp Cointreau

1 Preheat the oven to 200°C/400°F/ Gas 6. Grease and line a 33 x 23cm/ 13 x 9in Swiss roll tin with non-stick baking parchment.

2 Put the coffee in a bowl and pour the hot water over. Leave to infuse for about 4 minutes, then strain through a sieve.

3 Whisk the eggs and sugar together in a large bowl until pale and thick. Sift the flour over the mixture and fold in with the coffee and walnuts. Turn into the tin and bake for 10–12 minutes, until springy to the touch.

4 Turn out on a piece of greaseproof paper sprinkled with caster sugar, peel off the lining paper and cool for about 2 minutes. Trim the edges then roll up from one of the short ends, with the greaseproof paper where the filling will be. Leave to cool.

5 To make the filling, heat the sugar in the water over a low heat until dissolved. Boil rapidly until the syrup reaches 105°C/220°F on a sugar thermometer. Pour the syrup over the egg yolks, whisking all the time, until thick and mousse-like. Gradually add the butter, then whisk in the orange liqueur. Leave to cool and thicken.

6 Unroll the sponge and spread with the Cointreau cream. Re-roll and place on a serving plate seam-side down. Dust with extra caster sugar and chill in the fridge until ready to serve.

COOK'S TIP
Decorate the roll with swirls of piped whipped cream and walnuts, if you like.

COFFEE CHOCOLATE MOUSSE CAKE

SERVE THIS DENSE, DARK CHOCOLATE CAKE IN SMALL PORTIONS AS IT IS VERY RICH.

SERVES SIX

INGREDIENTS
    175g/6oz plain chocolate
    30ml/2 tbsp strong brewed coffee
    150g/5oz/10 tbsp butter, cubed
    50g/2oz/¼ cup caster sugar
    3 eggs
    25g/1oz/¼ cup ground almonds
    about 25ml/1½ tbsp icing sugar,
        for dusting
For the mascarpone and coffee cream
    250g/9oz/generous 1 cup mascarpone
    30ml/2 tbsp icing sugar, sifted
    30ml/2 tbsp strong brewed coffee

1 Preheat the oven to 200°C/400°F/Gas 6. Lightly grease and line the base of a 15cm/6in square tin with greaseproof paper.

2 Put the chocolate and coffee in a small heavy-based pan and heat very gently until melted, stirring occasionally.

3 Add the butter and sugar to the pan and stir until dissolved. Whisk the eggs until frothy and stir into the chocolate mixture with the ground almonds.

4 Pour into the prepared tin, then put in a large roasting tin and pour in enough hot water to come two-thirds up the cake tin. Bake for 50 minutes, or until the top feels springy to the touch. Leave to cool in the tin for 5 minutes, then turn the cake out upside-down on to a board and leave to cool.

5 Meanwhile, beat the mascarpone with the icing sugar and coffee. Dust the cake generously with icing sugar, then cut into slices. Serve on individual plates with the mascarpone and coffee cream alongside.

COOK'S TIP
The top of this flourless cake, with its moist mousse-like texture, will crack slightly as it cooks.

CAPPUCCINO TORTE

THE FAMOUS AND MUCH LOVED BEVERAGE OF FRESHLY BREWED COFFEE, WHIPPED CREAM, CHOCOLATE AND CINNAMON IS TRANSFORMED INTO A SENSATIONAL DESSERT.

SERVES SIX TO EIGHT

INGREDIENTS
    75g/3oz/6 tbsp butter, melted
    275g/10oz shortbread
        biscuits, crushed
    1.5ml/¼ tsp ground cinnamon
    25ml/1½ tbsp powdered gelatine
    45ml/3 tbsp cold water
    2 eggs, separated
    115g/4oz/½ cup soft light
        brown sugar
    115g/4oz plain chocolate, chopped
    175ml/6fl oz/¾ cup brewed espresso
    400ml/14fl oz/1⅔ cups
        whipping cream
    chocolate curls and ground
        cinnamon, to decorate

1 Mix the butter with the biscuits and cinnamon. Spoon into the base of a 20cm/8in loose-based tin and press down well. Chill in the fridge while making the filling.

2 Sprinkle the gelatine over the cold water. Leave to soften for 5 minutes, then place the bowl over a pan of hot water and stir to dissolve.

3 Whisk the egg yolks and sugar until thick. Put the chocolate in a bowl with the coffee and stir until melted. Add to the egg mixture, then cook gently in a pan for 1–2 minutes until thickened. Stir in the gelatine. Leave until just beginning to set, stirring occasionally.

4 Whip 150ml/¼ pint/⅔ cup of the cream until soft peaks form. Whisk the egg whites until stiff. Fold the cream into the coffee mixture, followed by the egg whites. Pour the mixture over the biscuit base and chill for 2 hours.

5 When ready to serve, remove the torte from the tin and transfer to a serving plate. Whip the remaining cream and place a dollop on top. Decorate with chocolate curls and a little cinnamon.

BAKED COFFEE CHEESECAKE

THIS RICH, COOKED AND CHILLED CHEESECAKE, FLAVOURED WITH COFFEE AND ORANGE LIQUEUR, HAS A WONDERFULLY DENSE, VELVETY TEXTURE.

SERVES EIGHT

INGREDIENTS
   45ml/3 tbsp near-boiling water
   30ml/2 tbsp ground coffee
   4 eggs
   225g/8oz/generous 1 cup
      caster sugar
   450g/1lb/2 cups cream cheese,
      at room temperature
   30ml/2 tbsp orange liqueur, such
      as Curaçao
   40g/1½oz/⅓ cup plain flour, sifted
   300ml/½ pint/1¼ cups
      whipping cream
   30ml/2 tbsp icing sugar, to dust
   single cream, to serve
For the base
   115g/4oz/1 cup plain flour
   5ml/1 tsp baking powder
   75g/3oz/6 tbsp butter
   50g/2oz/¼ cup caster sugar
   1 egg, lightly beaten
   30ml/2 tbsp cold water

1 Preheat the oven to 160°C/325°F/ Gas 3. Lightly grease and line a 20cm/8in loose-based tin with greaseproof paper.

2 Sift the flour and baking powder into a bowl. Rub in the butter until the mixture resembles fine breadcrumbs. Stir in the sugar, then add the egg and water and mix to a dough. Press the mixture into the base of the tin.

3 To make the filling, pour the water over the coffee and leave to infuse for 4 minutes. Strain through a fine sieve.

4 Whisk the eggs and sugar until thick. Using a wooden spoon, beat the cream cheese until softened, then beat in the liqueur, a spoonful at a time.

5 Gradually mix in the whisked eggs. Fold in the flour. Finally, stir in the whipping cream and coffee.

6 Pour the mixture over the base and bake in the oven for 1½ hours. Turn off the heat and leave in the oven to cool with the door ajar. Chill the cheesecake in the fridge for 1 hour. Dust the top with the icing sugar. Remove from the tin and place on a serving plate, Serve with single cream.

IRISH COFFEE CHEESECAKE

THE FLAVOURS OF WHISKEY, COFFEE AND GINGER GO WELL TOGETHER, BUT YOU CAN RING THE CHANGES BY USING ALMOND OR DIGESTIVE BISCUITS FOR THE BASE OF THIS CHEESECAKE.

SERVES EIGHT

INGREDIENTS
- 45ml/3 tbsp ground coffee
- 1 vanilla pod
- 250ml/8fl oz/1 cup single cream
- 15ml/1 tbsp powdered gelatine
- 45ml/3 tbsp cold water
- 450g/1lb/2 cups curd cheese, at room temperature
- 60ml/4 tbsp Irish whiskey liqueur, such as Millars or Irish Velvet
- 115g/4oz/½ cup soft light brown sugar
- 150ml/¼ pint/⅔ cup whipping cream

To decorate
- 150ml/¼ pint/⅔ cup whipping cream
- chocolate-covered coffee beans
- cocoa, for dusting

For the base
- 150g/5oz gingernut biscuits, finely crushed
- 25g/1oz/¼ cup toasted almonds, chopped
- 75g/3oz/6 tbsp butter, melted

1 To make the base, mix together the crushed gingernut biscuits, toasted almonds and melted butter and press firmly into the base of a 20cm/8in loose-based tin. Chill in the fridge.

2 Heat the coffee, vanilla and single cream in a pan to near-boiling point. Cover and leave to infuse for 15 minutes. Strain through a fine sieve. Sprinkle the gelatine over the water in a bowl and leave for 5 minutes. Place over a pan of simmering water until dissolved. Stir into the coffee cream.

3 Mix the curd cheese, liqueur and sugar together, then gradually blend in the coffee cream. Leave until just beginning to set.

4 Beat the whipping cream until soft peaks form, and fold into the coffee mixture. Spoon into the tin and chill for 3 hours, until set.

5 To decorate, whisk the whipping cream until soft peaks form and spread lightly over the top. Chill for at least 30 minutes, then transfer to a serving plate. Decorate with chocolate-covered coffee beans and cocoa.

VARIATION
Instead of a smooth layer of cream on top of the cheesecake, pipe swirls of cream around the edge of the cake.

PIES, TARTS AND PASTRIES

The flavour and aroma of real

coffee transforms perennial family

favourites into something special,

as you'll discover when you taste a

slice of Coffee Custard Tart or

Crunchy Topped Coffee Meringue

Pie. Along with these much-loved

pies and tarts are classic pastries

from around the world.

WALNUT PIE

Sweetened with coffee-flavoured maple syrup, this pie has a rich and sticky texture. The walnuts can be replaced by pecans for an authentic American pie.

SERVES EIGHT

INGREDIENTS
    30ml/2 tbsp ground coffee
    175ml/6 fl oz/¾ cup maple syrup
    25g/1oz/2 tbsp butter, softened
    175g/6oz/¾ cup soft light brown sugar
    3 eggs, beaten
    5ml/1 tsp vanilla extract
    115g/4oz/1 cup walnut halves
    crème fraîche or vanilla ice cream,
        to serve
For the pastry
    150g/5oz/1¼ cups plain flour
    pinch of salt
    25g/1oz/¼ cup golden icing sugar
    75g/3oz/6 tbsp butter, cubed
        and cubed
    2 egg yolks

1 Preheat the oven to 200°C/400°F/ Gas 6. To make the pastry, sift the flour, salt and icing sugar into a bowl. Rub in the butter until the mixture resembles fine breadcrumbs.

2 Add the egg yolks and mix to a dough. Turn out and knead on a lightly floured surface for a few seconds until smooth. Wrap in clear film and chill for 20 minutes.

3 Roll out the pastry and use to line a 20cm/8in fluted flan tin. Line with greaseproof paper and baking beans and bake for 10 minutes. Remove the paper and beans and bake for a further 5 minutes. Take out the pastry case and turn the oven to 180°C/350°F/Gas 4.

4 To make the filling, put the coffee and maple syrup in a small pan and heat until almost boiling. Remove from the heat and leave until just warm. Mix together the butter and sugar, then gradually beat in the eggs. Strain the maple syrup mixture through a fine sieve into the bowl and stir in with the vanilla extract.

5 Arrange the walnuts in the pastry case, then carefully pour in the filling. Bake for 30–35 minutes or until lightly browned and firm. Serve warm with crème fraîche or vanilla ice cream.

MISSISSIPPI PIE

THIS AMERICAN FAVOURITE WAS NAMED AFTER THE MUDDY BANKS OF THE MISSISSIPPI RIVER. IT HAS A DENSE LAYER OF CHOCOLATE MOUSSE, TOPPED WITH A MURKY COFFEE TOFFEE LAYER AND, FLOATING ON TOP, LOTS OF LOVELY FRESHLY WHIPPED CREAM.

SERVES EIGHT

INGREDIENTS

For the base
    275g/10oz digestive biscuits, crushed
    150g/5oz/10 tbsp butter, melted

For the chocolate layer
    10ml/2 tsp powdered gelatine
    30ml/2 tbsp cold water
    175g/6oz plain chocolate, broken
      into squares
    2 eggs, separated
    150ml/¼ pint/⅔ cup double cream

For the coffee toffee layer
    30ml/2 tbsp ground coffee
    300ml/½ pint/1¼ cups double cream
    200g/7oz/1 cup caster sugar
    25g/1oz/4 tbsp cornflour
    2 eggs, beaten
    15g/½oz/1 tbsp butter
    150ml/¼ pint/⅔ cup whipping cream
      and chocolate curls, to decorate

1 Grease a 21cm/8½in loose-based tin. Mix together the biscuit crumbs and butter and press over the base and sides of the tin. Chill for 30 minutes.

2 To make the chocolate layer, sprinkle the gelatine over the cold water and leave for 5 minutes. Put the bowl over a pan of hot water and stir until dissolved. Melt the chocolate in a bowl over hot water. Stir in the gelatine.

3 Blend the egg yolks and cream and stir into the chocolate. Whisk the egg whites and fold into the mixture. Pour into the biscuit case and chill for 2 hours.

4 To make the coffee layer, put the coffee in a bowl. Reserve 60ml/4 tbsp of cream. Heat the remaining cream to near-boiling and pour over. Leave to infuse for 4 minutes. Strain through a sieve back into the pan. Add the sugar and heat gently until dissolved.

5 Mix the cornflour with the reserved cream and the eggs. Add to the coffee and cream mixture and simmer gently for 2–3 minutes, stirring.

6 Stir in the butter and leave to cool for 30 minutes, stirring occasionally. Spoon over the chocolate layer. Chill in the fridge for 2 hours.

7 To make the topping, whip the cream until soft peaks form and spread thickly over the coffee toffee layer. Decorate with chocolate curls and chill until ready to serve.

CRUNCHY TOPPED COFFEE MERINGUE PIE

A SWEET PASTRY CASE IS FILLED WITH A COFFEE CUSTARD AND A MERINGUE TOPPING — CRISP AND GOLDEN ON THE OUTSIDE AND SOFT AND "MARSHMALLOWY" UNDERNEATH.

SERVES SIX TO EIGHT

INGREDIENTS
For the pastry
   175g/6oz/1½ cups plain flour
   15ml/1 tbsp icing sugar
   75g/3oz/6 tbsp butter
   1 egg yolk
   finely grated rind of ½ orange
   15ml/1 tbsp orange juice
For the filling
   30ml/2 tbsp ground coffee
   350ml/12fl oz/1½ cups milk
   25g/1oz/4 tbsp cornflour
   130g/4½ oz/½ cup caster sugar
   4 egg yolks
   15g/½ oz/1 tbsp butter
For the meringue
   3 egg whites
   1.5ml/¼ tsp cream of tartar
   150g/5oz/¾ cup caster sugar
   25g/1oz/¼ cup skinned hazelnuts
   15ml/1 tbsp demerara sugar

1 Preheat the oven to 200°C/400°F/ Gas 6. Sift the flour and icing sugar into a bowl. Rub in the butter until the mixture resembles breadcrumbs. Add the egg yolk, orange rind and juice and mix to a firm dough. Wrap in clear film and chill for 20 minutes. Roll out and use to line a 23cm/9in loose-based fluted flan tin. Cover with clear film and chill for 30 minutes.

COOK'S TIP
The pastry case can be made up to 36 hours in advance, but once filled and baked the pie should be eaten on the day of making.

2 Prick the pastry all over, line with greaseproof paper and baking beans and bake for 15 minutes, removing the paper and beans for the last 5 minutes. Turn the oven to 160°C/325°F/Gas 3.

3 To make the filling, put the coffee in a bowl. Heat 250ml/8fl oz/1 cup of the milk until near-boiling and pour over the coffee. Leave to infuse for 4 minutes, then strain. Blend the cornflour and sugar with the remaining milk in a pan and whisk in the coffee-flavoured milk.

4 Bring the mixture to the boil, stirring until thickened. Remove from the heat.

5 Beat the egg yolks. Stir in a little of the hot coffee mixture into the egg yolks, then add to the remaining coffee mixture with the butter. Cook the filling over a low heat for 3–4 minutes, until very thick. Pour into the pastry case.

6 To make the meringue, whisk the egg whites and cream of tartar until stiff. Whisk in the caster sugar a spoonful at a time.

7 Spoon the meringue over the filling and spread right to the edge of the pastry, swirling into peaks. Sprinkle with hazelnuts and demerara sugar and bake for 30–35 minutes, or until golden brown and crisp. Serve warm, or cool on a wire rack and serve cold.

COFFEE CUSTARD TART

A CRISP WALNUT PASTRY CASE, FLAVOURED WITH VANILLA, IS FILLED WITH A SMOOTH CREAMY COFFEE CUSTARD, BAKED UNTIL LIGHTLY SET AND TOPPED WITH CREAM.

SERVES SIX TO EIGHT

INGREDIENTS

1 vanilla pod
30ml/2 tbsp ground coffee
300ml/½ pint/1¼ cups single cream
150ml/¼ pint/⅔ cup milk
2 eggs, plus 2 egg yolks
50g/2oz/¼ cup caster sugar
icing sugar, for dusting
lightly whipped double cream,
  to serve

For the pastry

175g/6oz/1½ cups plain flour
30ml/2 tbsp icing sugar
115g/4oz/8 tbsp butter, cubed
75g/3oz/½ cup walnuts,
  finely chopped
1 egg yolk
5ml/1 tsp vanilla extract
10ml/2 tsp iced water

1 Preheat the oven to 200°C/400°F/ Gas 6. Put a baking sheet in the oven. Sift the flour and sugar into a bowl. Rub in the butter until the mixture resembles breadcrumbs. Stir in the walnuts. Mix together the egg yolk, vanilla and water. Add to the dry ingredients and mix to a dough. Wrap in clear film and chill for 20 minutes.

2 Roll out the dough and use to line a deep plain or fluted 20cm/8in flan ring, using a knife to smooth the edges. Chill again for 20 minutes. Prick the base with a fork. Fill with greaseproof paper and baking beans and bake on the hot baking sheet for 10 minutes. Remove the paper and beans and bake for a further 10 minutes. Turn the oven to 150°C/300°F/Gas 2.

3 Meanwhile, split the vanilla pod and scrape out the seeds. Put both in a pan with the coffee, cream and milk. Heat until near-boiling point, cover and infuse for 10 minutes. Whisk the eggs, egg yolks and caster sugar together.

4 Bring the cream back to boiling point and pour on to the egg mixture, stirring. Strain into the pastry case.

5 Bake the tart for 40–45 minutes or until lightly set. Take out of the oven and leave on a wire rack to cool. Remove the tart from the tin, pipe cream rosettes around the edge and dust with icing sugar to serve.

BLUEBERRY FRANGIPANE FLAN

A TANGY LEMON PASTRY CASE IS FILLED WITH A SWEET ALMOND FILLING DOTTED WITH RIPE
BLUEBERRIES. THE JAM AND LIQUEUR GLAZE ADDS AN INDULGENT FINISH.

SERVES SIX

INGREDIENTS
  30ml/2 tbsp ground coffee
  45ml/3 tbsp near-boiling milk
  50g/2oz/4 tbsp unsalted butter
  50g/2oz/¼ cup caster sugar
  1 egg
  115g/4oz/1 cup ground almonds
  15ml/1 tbsp plain flour, sifted
  225g/8oz/2 cups blueberries
  30ml/2 tbsp seedless
    blackberry jam
  15ml/1 tbsp liqueur, such as
    Amaretto or Cointreau
  mascarpone, crème fraîche or
    soured cream, to serve
For the pastry
  175g/6oz/1½ cups plain flour
  115g/4oz/8 tbsp unsalted butter
  25g/1oz/2 tbsp caster sugar
  finely grated rind of ½ lemon
  15ml/1 tbsp chilled water

1 Preheat the oven to 190°C/375°F/ Gas 5. Sift the flour into a bowl and rub in the butter. Stir in the sugar and lemon rind, then add the water and mix to a firm dough. Wrap in clear film and chill for 20 minutes.

2 Roll out the pastry on a lightly floured surface and use to line a 23cm/9in loose-based flan tin. Line the pastry with greaseproof paper and baking beans and bake for 10 minutes. Remove the paper and beans and bake for a further 10 minutes. Remove from the oven.

3 Meanwhile, to make the filling, put the coffee in a bowl. Pour the milk over and leave to infuse for 4 minutes. Cream the butter and sugar until pale. Beat in the egg, then add the almonds and flour. Strain in the coffee through a fine sieve and fold in.

COOK'S TIP
This flan can also be made in individual tartlets. Use six 10cm/4in tartlet tins and bake for 25 minutes.

4 Spoon the coffee mixture into the pastry case and spread evenly. Scatter the blueberries over the top and push them down slightly into the mixture. Bake for 30 minutes, until firm, covering with foil after 20 minutes.

5 Remove from the oven and allow to cool slightly. Heat the jam and liqueur in a small pan until melted. Brush over the flan and remove from the tin. Serve warm with a scoop of mascarpone or with crème fraîche or soured cream.

TIA MARIA TRUFFLE TARTS

THE IDEAL DESSERT FOR A TEA OR COFFEE BREAK, THESE MINI COFFEE PASTRY CASES ARE FILLED WITH A CHOCOLATE LIQUEUR TRUFFLE CENTRE AND TOPPED WITH FRESH RIPE BERRIES.

SERVES SIX

INGREDIENTS
    300ml/½ pint/1¼ cups double cream
    225g/8oz/generous ¾ cup seedless
      bramble or raspberry jam
    150g/5oz plain chocolate, broken
      into squares
    45ml/3 tbsp Tia Maria liqueur
    450g/1lb mixed berries, such as
      raspberries, small strawberries
      or blackberries
For the pastry
    225g/8oz/2 cups plain flour
    15ml/1 tbsp caster sugar
    150g/5oz/10 tbsp butter, cubed
    1 egg yolk
    30ml/2 tbsp very strong brewed
      coffee, chilled

1 Preheat the oven to 200°C/400°F/ Gas 6. Put a baking sheet in the oven to heat. To make the pastry, sift the flour and sugar into a large bowl. Rub in the butter. Stir the egg yolk and coffee together, add to the bowl and mix to a stiff dough. Knead lightly on a floured surface for a few seconds until smooth. Wrap in clear film and chill for about 20 minutes.

2 Use the pastry to line six 10cm/4in fluted tartlet tins. Prick the bases with a fork and line with greaseproof paper and baking beans. Put on the hot baking sheet and bake for 10 minutes. Remove paper and beans and bake for 8–10 minutes longer, until cooked. Cool on a wire rack.

3 To make the filling, slowly bring the cream and 175g/6oz/generous ½ cup of the jam to the boil, stirring continuously until dissolved.

COOK'S TIP
When making the pastry, blend the egg yolk and coffee together until well mixed to ensure an evenly coloured pastry.

4 Remove from the heat, add the chocolate and 30ml/2 tbsp of the liqueur. Stir until melted. Cool, then spoon into the pastry cases, and smooth the tops. Chill for 40 minutes.

5 Heat the remaining jam and liqueur until smooth. Arrange the fruit on top of the tarts, then brush the jam glaze over it. Chill until ready to serve.

COFFEE CREAM PROFITEROLES

CRISP-TEXTURED COFFEE CHOUX PASTRY PUFFS ARE FILLED WITH CREAM AND DRIZZLED WITH A WHITE CHOCOLATE SAUCE. FOR THOSE WITH A SWEET TOOTH, THERE IS PLENTY OF EXTRA SAUCE.

SERVES SIX

INGREDIENTS
  65g/2½oz/9 tbsp plain white flour
  pinch of salt
  50g/2oz/4 tbsp butter
  150ml/¼ pint/⅔ cup brewed coffee
  2 eggs, lightly beaten
For the white chocolate sauce
  50g/2oz/¼ cup sugar
  100ml/3½fl oz/scant ½ cup water
  150g/5oz good quality white dessert
    chocolate, broken into pieces
  25g/1oz/2 tbsp unsalted butter
  45ml/3 tbsp double cream
  30ml/2 tbsp coffee liqueur, such as
    Tia Maria, Kahlúa or Toussaint
To assemble
  250ml/8fl oz/1 cup double cream

1 Preheat the oven to 220°C/425°F/ Gas 7. Sift the flour and salt on to a piece of greaseproof paper. Cut the butter into pieces and put in a pan with the coffee.

2 Bring to a rolling boil, then remove from the heat and tip in all the flour. Beat until the mixture leaves the sides of the pan. Leave to cool for 2 minutes.

3 Gradually add the eggs, beating well between each addition. Spoon the mixture into a piping bag fitted with a 1cm/½in plain nozzle.

4 Pipe about 24 small buns on to a dampened baking sheet. Bake for 20 minutes, until well risen and crisp.

5 Remove the buns from the oven and pierce the side of each with a sharp knife to let out the steam.

6 To make the sauce, put the sugar and water in a heavy-based pan and heat gently until dissolved. Bring to the boil and simmer for 3 minutes. Remove from the heat. Add the chocolate and butter, stirring until smooth. Stir in the cream and liqueur.

7 To assemble, whip the cream until soft peaks form. Using a piping bag, fill the choux buns through the slits in the sides. Arrange on plates and pour a little of the sauce over, either warm or at room temperature. Serve the remaining sauce separately.

DANISH COFFEE PASTRIES

THESE WORLD FAMOUS CRISP PASTRIES ARE TIME-CONSUMING TO MAKE, BUT WELL WORTH THE EFFORT.

<u>MAKES SIXTEEN</u>

INGREDIENTS
   45ml/3 tbsp near-boiling water
   30ml/2 tbsp ground coffee
   115g/4oz/generous ½ cup
      caster sugar
   40g/1½ oz/3 tbsp unsalted butter
   1 egg yolk
   115g/4oz/1 cup ground almonds
   beaten egg, to glaze
   275g/10oz/1 cup apricot jam
   30ml/2 tbsp water
   175g/6oz/1½ cups icing sugar
   50g/2oz/½ cup flaked
      almonds, toasted
   50g/2oz/¼ cup glacé cherries
For the pastry
   275g/10oz/2½ cups plain flour
   1.5ml/¼ tsp salt
   15g/½oz/1 tbsp caster sugar
   225g/8oz/1 cup butter, softened
   10ml/2 tsp easy-blend dried yeast
   1 egg, beaten
   100ml/3½fl oz/scant ½ cup cold water

1 Sift the flour, salt and sugar into a bowl. Rub in 25g/1oz/2 tbsp butter. Stir in the yeast. Stir the egg and water, add to the bowl and mix to a soft dough. Lightly knead for 4–5 minutes. Put in a plastic bag and chill for 15 minutes.

2 Put the remaining butter between 2 sheets of greaseproof paper and beat with a rolling pin to make a 18cm/7in square. Roll out the dough to about 25cm/10in square. Put the butter in the middle, like a diamond, then bring up each corner of dough to fully enclose it.

3 Roll out the pastry to about 35cm/14in long. Turn up the bottom third of the pastry, then fold down the top third. Seal the edges together with a rolling pin. Return the pastry to the plastic bag and chill for 15 minutes.

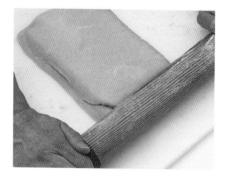

4 Repeat the rolling and folding three more times, each time turning the pastry so that the short ends are at the top and bottom. Allow a 15 minute rest between each turn.

5 To make the filling, pour the hot water over the coffee and infuse for 4 minutes. Strain through a fine sieve. Cream the sugar and butter together. Beat in the egg yolk, ground almonds and 15ml/1 tbsp of the coffee.

6 Divide the dough and filling equally into three. Roll one dough portion to an 18 x 35cm/7 x 14in rectangle. Spread with filling and roll up from a short end. Cut into six equal slices. Roll another portion into a 25cm/10in square; cut into a 25cm/10in round, remove the trimmings and cut into six segments.

7 Put a spoonful of filling at the widest end of each triangle, then roll up towards the point into a crescent.

8 Roll out the remaining dough into a 20cm/8in square; cut into four. Put some filling into the centre of each. Make cuts from each corner almost to the centre and fold four alternate points to the centre.

9 Preheat the oven to 220°C/425°F/Gas 7. Put the pastries on greased baking sheets, spaced apart. Cover loosely with oiled clear film and leave to rise for 20 minutes, until almost doubled in size. Brush with beaten egg and bake for 15–20 minutes, until lightly browned and crisp. Cool on wire racks.

10 Put the jam in a pan with the water; bring to the boil, then sieve. Brush the jam over the warm pastries. Mix the icing sugar with the remaining coffee, adding more water if necessary to make a thick icing. Drizzle the icing over some of the pastries and decorate some with flaked almonds or chopped glacé cherries. Leave to set before serving.

GREEK FRUIT AND NUT PASTRIES

AROMATIC SWEET PASTRY CRESCENTS, KNOWN AS "MOSHOPOUNGIA" IN GREECE, ARE PACKED WITH CANDIED CITRUS PEEL AND WALNUTS, SOAKED IN A COFFEE SYRUP.

MAKES SIXTEEN

INGREDIENTS
60ml/4 tbsp clear honey
60ml/4 tbsp strong brewed coffee
75g/3oz/½ cup mixed candied citrus peel, finely chopped
175g/6oz/1 cup walnuts, chopped
1.5ml/¼ tsp freshly grated nutmeg
milk, to glaze
caster sugar, for sprinkling
For the pastry
450g/1lb/4 cups plain flour
2.5ml/½ tsp ground cinnamon
2.5ml/½ tsp baking powder
pinch of salt
150g/5oz/10 tbsp unsalted butter
30ml/2 tbsp caster sugar
1 egg
120ml/4fl oz/½ cup chilled milk

1 Preheat the oven to 180°C/350°F/ Gas 4. To make the pastry, sift the flour, ground cinnamon, baking powder and salt into a bowl. Rub in the butter until the mixture resembles fine bread-crumbs. Stir in the sugar. Make a well in the middle.

2 Beat the egg and milk together and add to the well in the dry ingredients. Mix to a soft dough. Divide the dough into two and wrap each in clear film. Chill in the fridge for 30 minutes.

3 Meanwhile, to make the filling, mix the honey and coffee. Add the peel, walnuts and nutmeg. Stir well, cover and leave to soak for at least 20 minutes.

4 Roll out a portion of dough on a lightly floured surface until about 3mm/⅛in thick. Stamp out rounds using a 10cm/4in round cutter.

5 Place a heaped teaspoonful of filling on one side of each round. Brush the edges with a little milk, then fold over and press the edges together to seal. Repeat with remaining pastry until all the filling is used.

6 Put the pastries on lightly greased baking sheets, brush with milk and sprinkle with caster sugar.

7 Make a steam hole in each with a skewer. Bake for 35 minutes, or until lightly browned. Cool on a wire rack.

BAKLAVA

TURKISH COFFEE IS BLACK, THICK, VERY SWEET AND OFTEN SPICED. HERE IT IS USED IN THIS FAMOUS PASTRY CONFECTION, TRADITIONALLY SERVED ON RELIGIOUS FESTIVAL DAYS IN TURKEY.

MAKES SIXTEEN

INGREDIENTS
   50g/2oz/½ cup blanched
   almonds, chopped
   50g/2oz/½ cup pistachio
   nuts, chopped
   75g/3oz/scant ½ cup caster sugar
   115g/4oz filo pastry
   75g/3oz/6 tbsp unsalted butter,
   melted and cooled
For the syrup
   115g/4oz/generous ½ cup
   caster sugar
   7.5cm/3in piece cinnamon stick
   1 whole clove
   2 cardamom pods, crushed
   75ml/5 tbsp strong brewed coffee

1 Preheat the oven to 180°C/350°F/ Gas 4. Mix the nuts and sugar together. Cut the pastry to fit a tin measuring 18 x 28cm/7 x 11in. Brush the tin with a little butter. Lay a sheet of pastry in the tin and brush with melted butter.

2 Repeat with three more sheets and spread with half the nut mixture.

3 Layer up three more sheets of pastry, lightly brushing butter between the layers, then spread the remaining nut mixture over them, smoothing it over the entire surface. Top with the remaining pastry and butter. Gently press down the edges to seal.

4 With a sharp knife, mark the top into diamonds. Bake for 20–25 minutes until golden brown and crisp. Meanwhile, put the syrup ingredients in a small pan and heat gently until the sugar has dissolved. Cover with a lid and leave to infuse for 20 minutes.

5 Remove the baklava from the oven. Re-heat the syrup and strain over the pastry. Leave to cool in the tin. Cut into diamonds, remove from the tin and serve.

COOK'S TIP
While assembling the baklava, keep the pile of filo pastry covered with a damp cloth to stop it drying out and becoming brittle, which makes it difficult to use.

SWEETS, BISCUITS AND BREADS

Few people can resist the

tantalizing display of biscuits and

breads in the baker's shop window,

but it's easy to recreate those

delectable bakes at home. Here,

you'll find a selection of

traditional and Continental recipes

from rich and gooey truffles to a

stunning candied fruit plait.

STUFFED PRUNES

CHOCOLATE-COVERED PRUNES, SOAKED IN LIQUEUR, HIDE A MELT-IN-THE-MOUTH COFFEE FILLING.

MAKES APPROXIMATELY THIRTY

INGREDIENTS
    225g/8oz/1 cup unstoned prunes
    50ml/2fl oz/¼ cup Armagnac
    30ml/2 tbsp ground coffee
    150ml/¼ pint/⅔ cup double cream
    350g/12oz plain chocolate, broken
       into squares
    10g/¼oz/½ tbsp vegetable fat
    30ml/2 tbsp cocoa powder,
       for dusting

1 Put the unstoned prunes in a bowl and pour the Armagnac over. Stir, then cover with clear film and set aside for 2 hours, or until the prunes have absorbed the liquid.

COOK'S TIP
Fresh dates can be used instead of prunes, if preferred.

2 Make a slit along each prune to remove the stone, making a hollow for the filling, but leaving the fruit intact.

3 Put the coffee and cream in a pan and heat almost to boiling point. Cover, infuse for 4 minutes, then heat again until almost boiling. Put 115g/4oz of the chocolate into a bowl and pour over the coffee cream through a sieve.

4 Stir until the chocolate has melted and the mixture is smooth. Leave to cool, until it has the consistency of softened butter.

5 Fill a piping bag with a small plain nozzle with the chocolate mixture. Pipe into the cavities of the prunes. Chill in the fridge for 20 minutes.

6 Melt the remaining chocolate in a bowl over a pan of hot water. Using a fork, dip the prunes one at a time into the chocolate to give them a generous coating. Place on non-stick baking parchment to harden. Dust each with a little cocoa powder.

COFFEE CHOCOLATE TRUFFLES

BECAUSE THESE CLASSIC CHOCOLATES CONTAIN FRESH CREAM, THEY SHOULD BE STORED IN THE FRIDGE AND EATEN WITHIN A FEW DAYS.

MAKES TWENTY-FOUR

INGREDIENTS
  350g/12oz plain chocolate
  75ml/5 tbsp double cream
  30ml/2 tbsp coffee liqueur, such as
    Tia Maria, Kahlúa or Toussaint
  115g/4oz good quality white
    dessert chocolate
  115g/4oz good quality milk
    dessert chocolate

1 Melt 225g/8oz of the plain chocolate in a bowl over a pan of barely simmering water. Stir in the cream and liqueur, then chill the mixture in the fridge for 4 hours, until firm.

2 Divide the mixture into 24 equal pieces and quickly roll each into a ball. Chill for one more hour, or until they are firm again.

3 Melt the remaining plain, white and milk chocolate in separate small bowls. Using two forks, carefully dip eight of the truffles, one at a time, into the melted milk chocolate.

4 Repeat with the white and plain chocolate. Place the truffles on a board, covered with wax paper or foil. Leave to set before removing and placing in a serving bowl or individual paper cases.

VARIATIONS
Ring the changes by adding one of the following to the truffle mixture:
Ginger – Stir in 40g/1½oz/¼ cup finely chopped crystallized ginger.
Candied fruit – Stir in 50g/2oz/⅓ cup finely chopped candied fruit, such as pineapple and orange.
Pistachio – Stir in 25g/1oz/¼ cup, chopped skinned pistachio nuts.
Hazelnut – Roll each ball of chilled truffle mixture around a whole skinned hazelnut.
Raisin – Soak 40g/1½oz/generous ¼ cup raisins overnight in 15ml/1 tbsp coffee liqueur, such as Tia Maria or Kahlúa and stir into the truffle mixture.

CHOCOLATE <u>AND</u> COFFEE MINT THINS

THESE COFFEE-FLAVOURED CHOCOLATE SQUARES CONTAIN PIECES OF CRISP MINTY CARAMEL AND ARE IDEAL FOR SERVING WITH AFTER-DINNER COFFEE.

MAKES SIXTEEN

INGREDIENTS
    75g/3oz/scant ½ cup sugar
    75ml/5 tbsp water
    3 drops oil of peppermint
    15ml/1 tbsp strong-flavoured
      ground coffee
    75ml/5 tbsp near-boiling
      double cream
    225g/8oz plain chocolate
    10g/¼oz/½ tbsp unsalted butter

COOK'S TIP
Don't put the chocolate in the fridge to set, or it may loose its glossy appearance and become too brittle to cut easily into neat squares.

1 Line a 18cm/7in square tin with non-stick baking parchment. Gently heat the sugar and water in a heavy-based pan until dissolved. Add the peppermint, and boil until a light caramel colour.

2 Pour the caramel on to an oiled baking sheet and leave to harden, then crush into small pieces.

3 Put the coffee in a small bowl and pour the hot cream over. Leave to infuse for about 4 minutes, then strain through a fine sieve. Melt the chocolate and unsalted butter in a bowl over barely simmering water. Remove from the heat and beat in the hot coffee cream. Stir in the mint caramel.

4 Pour the mixture into the prepared tin and smooth the surface level. Leave in a cool place to set for at least 4 hours, preferably overnight.

5 Carefully turn out the chocolate on to a board and peel off the lining paper. Cut the chocolate into squares with a sharp knife and store in an airtight container until needed.

COFFEE <u>AND</u> HAZELNUT MACAROONS

MACAROONS ARE TRADITIONALLY MADE WITH GROUND ALMONDS. THIS RECIPE USES HAZELNUTS, WHICH ARE LIGHTLY ROASTED BEFORE GRINDING, BUT YOU CAN USE WALNUTS INSTEAD, IF PREFERRED.

MAKES TWENTY

INGREDIENTS
    edible rice paper
    115g/4oz/⅔ cup skinned hazelnuts
    225g/8oz/generous 1 cup
      caster sugar
    15ml/1 tbsp ground rice
    10ml/2 tsp ground coffee,
      e.g. hazelnut-flavoured
    2 egg whites
    caster sugar, for sprinkling

1 Preheat the oven to 180°C/350°F/ Gas 4. Line two baking sheets with rice paper. Place the skinned hazelnuts on a baking sheet and cook for 5 minutes. Cool, then place in a food processor and grind until fine.

2 Mix the ground nuts with the sugar, ground rice and coffee. Stir in the egg whites to make a fairly stiff paste.

3 Spoon into a piping bag fitted with a 1cm/½in plain nozzle. Pipe rounds on the rice paper, leaving room to spread.

4 Sprinkle each macaroon with a little caster sugar then bake for 20 minutes, or until pale golden in colour. Transfer to a wire rack to cool. Remove excess rice paper when completely cold. Serve immediately or store in an airtight tin for up to 2–3 days.

COFFEE AND MACADAMIA MUFFINS

THESE MUFFINS ARE DELICIOUS EATEN COLD, BUT ARE BEST SERVED STILL WARM FROM THE OVEN.

MAKES TWELVE

INGREDIENTS
    25ml/1½ tbsp ground coffee
    250ml/8fl oz/1 cup milk
    50g/2oz/4 tbsp butter
    275g/10oz/2½ cups plain flour
    10ml/2 tsp baking powder
    150g/5oz/10 tbsp light
      muscovado sugar
    75g/3oz/½ cup macadamia nuts
    1 egg, lightly beaten

1 Preheat the oven to 200°C/400°F/
Gas 6. Lightly grease a 12-hole muffin
or a deep-bun tray with oil. Alternatively,
line with paper muffin cases.

2 Put the coffee in a jug or bowl. Heat
the milk to near-boiling and pour it over.
Leave to infuse for 4 minutes, then
strain through a sieve.

3 Add the butter to the coffee-
flavoured milk mixture and stir until
melted. Leave until cold.

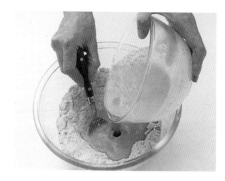

4 Sift the flour and baking powder into
a large mixing bowl. Stir in the sugar
and macadamia nuts. Add the egg to
the coffee-flavoured milk mixture, pour
into the dry ingredients and stir until
just combined – do not over-mix.

5 Divide the coffee mixture between
the prepared muffin cases and bake for
about 15 minutes until well risen and
firm. Transfer to a wire rack and serve
warm or cold.

COOK'S TIP
To cool the coffee-flavoured milk quickly,
place the jug in a large bowl of iced or
cold water.

CHUNKY WHITE CHOCOLATE AND COFFEE BROWNIES

*BROWNIES SHOULD HAVE A GOOEY TEXTURE, SO TAKE CARE NOT TO OVERCOOK THEM — WHEN READY,
THE MIXTURE WILL STILL BE SLIGHTLY SOFT UNDER THE CRUST, BUT WILL FIRM AS IT COOLS.*

MAKES TWELVE

INGREDIENTS
    25ml/1½ tbsp ground coffee
    45ml/3 tbsp near-boiling water
    300g/11oz plain chocolate, broken
      into pieces
    225g/8oz/1 cup butter
    225g/8oz/1 cup caster sugar
    3 eggs
    75g/3oz/⅔ cup self-raising
      flour, sifted
    225g/8oz white chocolate, chopped

1 Preheat the oven to 190°C/375°F/
Gas 5. Grease and line the base of a
18 x 28cm/7 x 11in tin with greaseproof
paper. Put the coffee in a bowl and
pour the water over. Leave to infuse for
4 minutes, then strain through a sieve.

2 Put the plain chocolate and butter in
a bowl over a pan of hot water and stir
occasionally until melted. Remove from
the heat and cool for 5 minutes.

3 Mix the sugar and eggs together. Stir
in the chocolate and butter mixture and
the coffee. Stir in the sifted flour.

4 Fold in the white chocolate pieces.
Pour into the prepared tin.

5 Bake for 45–50 minutes, or until firm
and the top is crusty. Leave to cool in
the tin. When completely cold, cut into
squares and remove from the tin.

PECAN TOFFEE SHORTBREAD

COFFEE SHORTBREAD IS TOPPED WITH PECAN-STUDDED TOFFEE. CORNFLOUR GIVES IT A CRUMBLY LIGHT TEXTURE, BUT ALL PLAIN FLOUR CAN BE USED IF YOU LIKE.

MAKES TWENTY

INGREDIENTS
    15ml/1 tbsp ground coffee
    15ml/1 tbsp near-boiling water
    115g/4oz/8 tbsp butter, softened
    30ml/2 tbsp smooth peanut butter
    75g/3oz/scant ½ cup caster sugar
    75g/3oz/⅔ cup cornflour
    185g/6½oz/1⅔ cups plain flour
For the topping
    175g/6oz/12 tbsp butter
    175g/6oz/¾ cup soft light
      brown sugar
    30ml/2 tbsp golden syrup
    175g/6oz/1 cup shelled pecan nuts,
      roughly chopped

1 Preheat the oven to 180°C/350°F/
Gas 4. Lightly grease and line the base
of a 18 x 28cm/7 x 11in tin with
greaseproof paper.

2 Put the ground coffee in a small bowl
and pour the hot water over. Leave to
infuse for 4 minutes, then strain through
a fine sieve.

3 Cream the butter, peanut butter,
sugar and coffee together until light.
Sift the cornflour and flour together and
mix in to make a smooth dough.

4 Press into the base of the tin and prick
all over with a fork. Bake for 20 minutes.
To make the topping, put the butter,
sugar and syrup in a pan and heat until
melted. Bring to the boil.

5 Allow to simmer for 5 minutes, then
stir in the chopped nuts. Spread the
topping over the base. Leave in the tin
until cold, then cut into fingers. Remove
from the tin and serve.

COFFEE BISCOTTI

THESE CRISP BISCUITS ARE MADE TWICE AS DELICIOUS WITH BOTH FRESHLY ROASTED GROUND COFFEE BEANS AND STRONG AROMATIC BREWED COFFEE IN THE MIXTURE.

MAKES ABOUT THIRTY

INGREDIENTS
25g/1oz/⅓ cup espresso-roasted
   coffee beans
115g/4oz/⅔ cup blanched almonds
200g/7oz/scant 2 cups plain flour
7.5ml/1½ tsp baking powder
1.5ml/¼ tsp salt
75g/3oz/6 tbsp unsalted butter, cubed
150g/5oz/¾ cup caster sugar
2 eggs, beaten
25–30ml/1½–2 tbsp strong
   brewed coffee
5ml/1 tsp ground cinnamon,
   for dusting

1 Preheat the oven to 180°C/350°F/ Gas 4. Put the espresso coffee beans in a single layer on one side of a large baking sheet and the almonds on the other. Roast in the oven for 10 minutes. Leave to cool.

2 Put the coffee beans in a blender or food processor and process until fairly fine. Tip out and set aside. Process the almonds until finely ground.

3 Sift the flour, baking powder and salt into a bowl. Rub in the butter until the mixture resembles fine breadcrumbs. Stir in the caster sugar, ground coffee and almonds. Add the beaten eggs and enough brewed coffee to make a fairly firm dough.

COOK'S TIP
Store the biscotti in an airtight tin for at least a day before serving.

4 Lightly knead for a few seconds until smooth and shape into two rolls about 7.5cm/3in in diameter. Place on a greased baking sheet and dust with cinnamon. Bake for 20 minutes.

5 Using a sharp knife, cut the rolls into 4cm/1½in slices on the diagonal. Arrange the slices on the baking tray and bake for a further 10 minutes, or until lightly browned. Cool on a rack.

CAPPUCCINO PANETTONE

THIS LIGHT BREAD IS SERVED IN ITALY AS PART OF THEIR CHRISTMAS FARE. IT'S TRADITIONALLY A TALL LOAF WITH A DOME ON THE TOP, FORMED BY THE RICH YEASTED DOUGH AS IT RISES.

SERVES EIGHT

INGREDIENTS

450g/1lb/4 cups strong plain flour
2.5ml/½ tsp salt
75g/3oz/scant ½ cup caster sugar
7g/¼oz sachet easy-blend
  dried yeast
115g/4oz/8 tbsp butter
100ml/3½fl oz/scant ½ cup very hot
  strong brewed espresso coffee
100ml/3½fl oz/½ cup milk
4 egg yolks
115g/4oz/⅔ cup plain
  chocolate chips
beaten egg, to glaze

1 Preheat the oven to 190°C/375°F/ Gas 5. Lightly grease and line a deep 14–15cm/5½–6in cake tin with greaseproof paper. Sift the flour and salt into a large bowl. Stir in the sugar and yeast.

2 Add the butter to the coffee and stir until melted. Stir in the milk, then add to the dry ingredients with the egg yolks. Mix together to make a dough.

COOK'S TIP
Unlike commercial varieties, home-made panettone should be eaten within a day or two of baking.

3 Turn the dough out on to a lightly floured surface and knead for 10 minutes, until smooth and elastic. Knead in the chocolate chips.

4 Shape into a ball, place in the tin and cover with oiled clear film. Leave to rise in a warm place for 1 hour or until the dough reaches the top of the tin. Lightly brush with beaten egg and bake for 35 minutes.

5 Turn down the oven to 180°C/350°F/ Gas 4 and cover the panettone with foil if it has browned enough. Cook for a further 10–15 minutes, or until done.

6 Allow the panettone to cool in the tin for 10 minutes, then transfer to a wire rack. Remove the lining paper just before slicing and serving.

CANDIED FRUIT BREAD

THE CENTRE OF THIS COFFEE-FLAVOURED YEASTED PLAIT CONTAINS BRIGHTLY COLOURED CANDIED FRUITS, MOISTENED BY SOAKING IN RICH COFFEE LIQUEUR.

SERVES SIX TO EIGHT

INGREDIENTS
175g/6oz/1 cup mixed candied fruit,
    such as pineapple, orange and
    cherries, chopped
60ml/4 tbsp coffee liqueur, such as
    Tia Maria, Kahlúa or Toussaint
30ml/2 tbsp ground coffee
100ml/3½fl oz/½ cup
    near-boiling milk
225g/8oz/2 cups strong plain flour
1.5ml/¼ tsp salt
25g/1oz/2 tbsp soft light brown sugar
½ x 7g/¼oz sachet easy-blend
    dried yeast
1 egg, beaten
50g/2oz white almond paste, grated
65g/2½oz/¼ cup apricot jam
15g/½oz/1 tbsp unsalted butter
15ml/1 tbsp caster sugar
15ml/1 tbsp clear honey

1 Put the candied fruit in a small bowl and spoon the coffee liqueur over. Stir to coat the fruit, then cover with clear film and leave to soak overnight.

2 Preheat the oven to 200°C/400°F/ Gas 6. Put the coffee in a bowl; pour the hot milk over and leave until tepid. Strain through a fine sieve. Sift the flour and salt into a bowl. Stir in the brown sugar and yeast. Make a well in the centre, add the coffee-flavoured milk and the egg and mix to a soft dough.

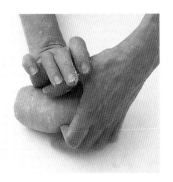

3 Knead for 10 minutes. Put the dough in a clean bowl, cover with clear film and leave to rise for 1 hour.

4 Meanwhile, mix the soaked fruit, almond paste and jam together. Lightly knead the dough again for 1 minute, then roll out to a rectangle 35 x 30cm/ 14 x 12in.

5 Spread the filling in a 7.5cm/3in strip lengthways down the middle to within 5cm/2in of each end. Make 14 diagonal cuts about 2cm/¾in wide in the dough either side of the filling.

6 Fold the ends of the dough up over the filling, overlapping alternate strips, Tuck in the last two strips neatly. Place on a greased baking tray.

7 Cover with clear film and leave to rise for 20 minutes. Melt the butter, sugar and honey in a small pan, then brush over the braid. Bake for 20–25 minutes. Allow to cool before slicing and serving.

INDEX